USING PERSONAL COMPUTERS IN THE CHURCH

KENNETH BEDELL

Judson Press ® Valley Forge

USING PERSONAL COMPUTERS IN THE CHURCH

Copyright © 1982
Judson Press, Valley Forge, PA 19481

Apple™ and APPLE WRITER™ are trademarks of Apple Computers.
Commodore PET 2001™, Commodore CBM 4032™, and PET™ are trademarks of Commodore Business Machines, Inc.
DS990™ is a trademark of Texas Instruments, Inc.
Explorer/85™ is a trademark of Netronics Research and Development, Ltd.
INCHURCH 80™ is a trademark of Membership Services, Inc.
JINSAM™ is a trademark of Jini Micro-Systems, Inc.
OpScan™ is a trademark of National Computer Services.
PASCAL™ is a trademark of U.C.S.D. Regents.
SCRIPSIT/DISK™, MICROFILES™, and TRS-80™ are trademarks of Tandy Corporation.
Selectric™ is a trademark of International Business Machines, Inc.
SOURCE™ is a trademark of Source Telecomputing Corporation.
Starwriter™ is a trademark of C. Ithol Electronics, Inc.
Vector Graphic System B™ is a trademark of Vector Graphic, Inc.
VISICALC™ is a trademark of Personal Software, Inc.
WORD PRO™ is a trademark of Professional Software, Inc.
WS 78™ is a trademark of Digital Equipment Corporation.
Z-2H™ is a trademark of Cromemco™, Inc.

The purchase of this book includes license for single personal use of software included in the appendices. Other duplication or distribution is prohibited without the permission of the authors of each program.

Library of Congress Cataloging in Publication Data
Bedell, Kenneth B.
  Using personal computers in the church.

  Bibliography: p.
  1. Church management—Data processing.   2. Computers.
I. Title.
BV652.77.B4   254'.0028'54   82-34
ISBN 0-8170-0948-5   AACR2

Acknowledgment

Dedicated to LESTER SCHAFF

The assistance of many individuals is evident throughout the book. To each, a sincere thanks is offered. The assistance of six people not mentioned in the text was also invaluable. Felton May, Samuel Pizzigati, Becky Turner, Sara Storm, Richard Bailey, and Kathryn Bedell: thank you all.

Prices and technical information have been provided for their educational value. Every effort has been made to supply accurate information. However, technical characteristics and prices are subject to rapid change. Manufacturers reserve the right to change circuitry and prices at any time without notice. The manufacturers' data should be consulted for exact specifications.

Contents

List of Figures

Introduction

We live in a world that is becoming dependent on *computers*.[1] In some areas of society computers have been introduced with little disruption occurring. Most of us, however, can tell a story about a time when a computer used by the government, a bank, or a business has caused us frustration and inconvenience. Not surprisingly, then, we greet with mixed feelings the idea that computers are on the verge of changing the way ministry is practiced. But computers cannot be avoided. And the truth is that they will greatly facilitate the work of the church.

Computers are already being used indirectly by every minister and church and directly by some. Computers were used in the production of this book and are used in making most other books we read today! Banks supply accurate statements for church accounts using computer technology. In fact, every time a minister makes a telephone call, the church benefits from computer technology.

We accept the idea of government and business benefiting from computers, but we don't want to see the church become impersonal or treat people only as numbers and *data*. In the church a high value is placed on the quality of relationships. So, for us, the important question becomes: How can computers become part of the life of the church in such a way that they benefit ministry? Part of the answer is that computers can help the church to respond more sensitively to the needs of individuals. They can help with the tedious, time-consuming chores so

---

[1] Throughout the book terms which are included in the glossary will be *italicized* at their first use.

that more time is available for creative work and involvement with people.

Entering the Computer Age

Most churches use cassette recorders in one way or another. Some ministers use these recorders to dictate correspondence that is later typed by a church secretary. Others listen to sermons or lectures on cassettes. The cassette recorder has provided the opportunity to adapt technology to the individual needs of each congregation. It has also offered the opportunity for creative new ministries, such as making worship service tapes to distribute to shut-ins.

In the same way the computer offers the potential for adaptation to the individual needs of each church and to the gifts of each minister. Just as cassette recorders do not have one uniform application in ministry, so computers will not be used in the same way in every church.

To help the church move into the computer age, ministers and other workers in the church need to develop an understanding of the potential and the limits of the computer. People in the church do not need to become experts in electronic engineering, nor do they need to be able to write *instructions* that direct the internal operation of the computer. They *do* need to be familiar, however, with what a computer can and cannot do.

Ivor Catt, a disillusioned computer engineer, has observed in his book *Computer Worship* that few people really understand computers. "My experience is typical of the industry as a whole," writes Catt, "and it is of computers being sold by salesmen who know little about their products to customers who know even less."[2]

To avoid investing money and time in computers that will not help with ministry, it is necessary for you to be able to do these three things:

1. Identify areas in your ministry where a computer can contribute.
2. Evaluate computer equipment to determine what equipment will meet your needs.
3. Understand the role of instructions (called *software*) used by the computer and know how to obtain and evaluate software.

The purpose of this book is to introduce computers so that your church can wisely move into the computer age.

Avoiding Disappointment and Problems

Understanding the uses of computers, computer equipment, and com-

[2]Ivor Catt, *Computer Worship* (London: Pitman Publishers, 1973), p. 83.

puter software (computer programs) will help you move into the computer age. This understanding is also important so that you will be able to avoid becoming a victim of computer technology.

Figure 1—1   TI-99/4 personal computer.
(Courtesy of Texas Instruments, Incorporated.)

Computers have many possible uses that would be inappropriate in the church just as cassette recorders have possible but inappropriate uses. It would be unthinkable, although technically possible, for a minister to prerecord Sunday's sermon and play it from a cassette recorder sitting on the pulpit while he or she went home for a second cup of coffee. In the same way, it would be possible to have a computer dial the telephone number of each church member early Sunday morning with a reminder to get up for church and a message about how the family is keeping up with its pledge. It is a possible use—but an inappropriate one.

Most decisions about computer use will be more difficult than whether to wake people up for church with computers. Sometimes it will be necessary to decide whether the use is worth the cost of having a computer accomplish a certain task, such as the updating of a mailing list. At other times a computer may reduce the need for volunteer help or even paid staff. Computer applications will need to be carefully evaluated, also, to determine whether the results justify the work necessary to make the computer system operate. The cost versus the benefits, keeping in mind the positive and negative effects on work patterns, will always need to be carefully evaluated.

In every case great care must be taken to obtain computer equipment that is appropriate for the task you expect the computer to do. Equipment can be inappropriate either because it is not large enough to meet your needs or because it is too sophisticated and large for the task at hand. Computer buyers also need to consider their future needs.

The success of every computer application depends on the quality of the software—the set of instructions that guide the operation of the computer. The test of software is the ease with which it facilitates the use of the computer and the accomplishing of a desired task. Every user can be an expert on whether a computer system with its software is useful and simple.

Asking computers to accomplish tasks for which they are not suited, depending on equipment that cannot accomplish a desired task, investing in more equipment than is necessary, being unable to make the computer function according to expectations—these are all problems that can and should be avoided.

Finding a Computer System

When a worker in the church needs automobile transportation to accomplish the work of the church, he or she has three options: hiring a taxi, renting a car, or purchasing a car. Just as most ministers have decided that owning a car makes the most sense, so most ministers will decide to own a computer. Computers can also be used in ways that parallel hiring a taxi or renting a car and these options should be carefully examined before purchasing a computer.

Computer services are the taxis of the computer world. When a computer service is used, the computer is never seen by the user. Information is delivered to the computer service and the results are returned. The major advantage of the computer service is that everything is provided. Just as one does not need to know how to drive in order to ride in a taxi, so one does not need to understand how a computer works in order to use a computer service.

One service that computer services do very well is to prepare self-adhesive mailing labels. To use this service, the church sends in a list of names and addresses and, for a set fee, address labels can be prepared. The names can be coded for use on special mailing lists. There is a charge each time a name or address is changed. It may take a computer several minutes to accomplish the task that would take an hour or more of changing and sorting addresses by hand on a variety of separately kept lists in a church office. If preparing mailing labels is the only task for which a computer will be used, buying your own computer is not cost effective.

Computer services might also be contracted with in order to control church finances or to accomplish a unique task such as evaluating census data.

A second way to use a computer is with a *time-sharing* system. This is like using a rented car: it is necessary to know how to use the equipment and the equipment can be rented for only the time that it is going to be used. With a time-sharing system the user has a *terminal* (owned or rented by the user) that looks like a television set with a typewriter keyboard attached. This screen and *keyboard* combination, called a "*CRT* terminal," is connected through a telephone line to the main computer. Computers can provide services to a number of users at once so that each user is given the impression that he or she is the only person getting computer service. Companies that offer time-sharing facilities often rent the use of the terminal, the computer time, and the software. Some time-sharing companies work very closely with customers to provide software and assistance with computer problems. Other companies rent computer time but do not provide very much support.

The advantage of time-sharing is that it makes it unnecessary to invest in computer equipment beyond a terminal and telephone connection—and even these can be rented. The computer, in addition, need be paid for only when in use. Some time-sharing systems offer other advantages, such as the ability to share information with other users or instant access to current information such as news bulletins or airline schedules. These services do not involve computations. They are telecommunications services which use a computer terminal to send and receive information. Time-sharing systems differ from computer services in that with the former the operation of the computer is left up to you.

Today owning a computer is not only possible but usually is also the best way for churches and ministers to benefit from computer technology. Personal computer systems cost very little to operate and maintain and can be purchased for under $4,000. Over a long period of time the cost of equipment and maintenance will probably be less than the cost of telephone service for the church and far less than the expense of providing transportation for church work. The church cannot afford to postpone benefiting from computer technology.

Personal computers are self-contained computers that have the potential of doing all the computing that can be done by computer services or time-sharing systems. Owning a personal computer is like owning an automobile. When you want to use it, it is there waiting for you.

The ownership of a personal computer offers opportunities for creative application of computer technology to the tasks of ministry. Once the computer has been purchased, using it for additional tasks is almost free.

The focus of this book is personal computers.

In the future personal computers will become tools as useful for churches and ministers as automobiles and cassette recorders are today. As you will see in reading the following chapters, inexpensive computer systems are already available to make that future possible in your ministry today.

Computers in the Church   2

Computers are an advancement in the technology related to the production, use, and manipulation of symbols. Computers follow the invention of pencils, printing presses, and typewriters as aids in using symbols. Whereas pencils, printing presses, and typewriters aid in producing symbols, computers facilitate the use and manipulation of symbols.

What can computers do? The answer is very simple. Computers produce, recognize, compare, and modify electronic symbols very rapidly. This means that any task which the computer can do could also be accomplished by writing symbols on a piece of paper and modifying them. The only difference is that the computer is capable of producing, recognizing, comparing, and modifying symbols very quickly.

Two numbers can be added by a computer in as little as one-millionth of a second. Because the process of adding with a computer involves obtaining the numbers to be added and storing them again as well as clarifying the instructions, most personal computers do not do one million additions in a second. However, even a personal computer adds several hundred numbers in a second. The speed with which computers are able to manipulate symbols makes them useful tools.

Computers can also work with very large amounts of information. An electronic device smaller than your thumb can store symbols which represent the text of a Sunday sermon. Over fifty pages of typed material can be stored on a disk which is five inches in diameter and paper thin. Because information can be stored in a small space, computers can be used to evaluate large amounts of information.

Any task that can be accomplished using symbols can be done with the help of a computer. Because many of the tasks performed by ministers and other church workers involve symbols as either written words or numbers, the computer offers an opportunity to increase the speed and accuracy with which these tasks can be accomplished. The computer may also make some neglected or difficult tasks easier to do.

Computers Make Old Tasks Easier

The tedious jobs of keeping records and accounts in a church office are obvious candidates for computer assistance.

The banking industry has demonstrated the efficiency and benefits of having computers help with record keeping. Any system of record keeping depends upon the accurate entry of information. In this a computer system is no different from a system that does not use computers. However, a computer makes the tedious jobs of copying information and making calculations unnecessary; this work is all done by the computer according to a predetermined series of steps.

Several churches are using personal computers to keep church accounts. Receipts and expenditures along with codes indicating the sources of receipts and the categories of expenditure are entered into the computer. The computer automatically keeps totals of expenses in budget categories and provides total receipts from each source. The computer can also prepare regular reports and examine the data for changing patterns or dangerous symptoms. For example, the computer might indicate when an expense entered is approaching or exceeding certain budget limits. Or it might analyze receipts from regular contributors to determine if there are changes in the giving pattern and thus signal the need for a pastoral call.

Computers bring speed and accuracy to church accounts. They seldom make mistakes when accurate information is correctly entered. In some cases the computer can even watch for common human errors and call attention to possible error. For example, the computer might automatically question every expenditure over $2,000.

Once a computer accounting system has been set up, the only time it demands is the time necessary to enter information. The production of financial statements for contributors and reports of expenditures is done automatically by the computer.

The Internal Revenue Service has developed a sophisticated computerized storage system to keep track of records and statistics which come from a number of different sources. A church might also benefit from computer storage and organization of statistical and membership information. The primary advantage of using a computer rather than a book or card filing system is that the computer can provide very rapid access to information, can easily update information, and can organize the information as needed. Each update automatically corrects the appropriate statistics so that accurate statistical information is always available.

It is not necessary to decide in advance the most useful way to have the information presented. A computer that has been given the names, birthdays, and baptism dates of parishioners can present one list of names in alphabetical order, another list according to the age of members, and a third list according to baptism dates. Or the list of members can be searched to determine all those who have been members for more than fifty years. Attendance records can also be stored in a computer.

The use of computers to keep accurate and up-to-date mailing lists was one of the first cost-effective business applications of computers. Churches could likewise benefit from computer technology in this area although they offer special problems for mailing list control. Most churches have several lists; for example, the list of church officers is probably kept separately from the list used for mailing a newsletter. Sometimes each list is kept by a different person. When a member moves, his or her address must be changed not only on the master list but also on a number of other lists.

A computer can simplify this job by keeping a centralized mailing list. With each entry a code can be included that indicates on which individual lists the name should appear. Or the computer can store information about the makeup of various groups in the church and create an accurate mailing list for a group anytime one is needed. Moreover, each time an address is changed, the computer insures that all lists are corrected. A computer list can be quickly reorganized as well. For example, one time the list can be printed in alphabetical order, another time in zip code order.

The Library of Congress has developed a computerized catalogue system that makes it easier to find books and articles in the library's large collection. The system is organized very much like a library card catalogue. When a particular author, title, or subject is entered into the computer, the computer returns an alphabetical list of the general groupings of books which are closest to the word which was entered. When asked, the computer will display the titles and authors of any group of books. In some cases there is additional information about specific books that can be examined. The Library of Congress system includes books that are not in the library's collection which makes it an ideal tool for developing bibliographies.

Even a much smaller church library or personal library of a minister can benefit from the organization made possible with computers. If title, author, subject, key words, publisher, and date are all entered into the computer, it is possible not only to discover what books are in the library written by a certain author but also to discover what books published since a given date on a particular subject are in the library. If information about borrowed library books is kept in the computer, it is possible to provide a list each month of those who have not returned the books on time.

Word processing is an area of computer application that is becoming very popular and has many applications in a church. Word processing simply means using a computer to help produce written material. Written words are typed on a terminal keyboard and are instantly viewed on a screen or *monitor*. The computer can be instructed to remove or add words as well as to correct spelling and other errors. Some computer systems check the spelling of every word using a dictionary listing that is stored in the computer. It is also possible to have the computer automatically perform editing functions, such as changing the word "pastor" in every case to "minister." The computer can search through a document to find a certain passage or word and can make changes in the text that is visible on the screen without destroying the actual text.

The computer can also organize the format for printing of the text on paper. For example, a sermon could be printed with double spacing for use in the pulpit and later be printed with single spacing to send to a parishioner in the hospital. A form letter can be written into which the computer will automatically insert names or other specific information. A letter about church finances could selectively include a paragraph thanking those who have paid their pledges while leaving that paragraph out in letters sent to people who have fallen behind.

Word processing can also be a helpful tool in the preparation of material for newsletter or bulletin announcements. Information for a newsletter is entered into the computer where it is stored. Instead of the usual "cut and paste" approach, editing can be done as the computer manipulates words on a screen.

All ministers have their own system of writing sermons. The computer offers the potential for contributing to whatever system is used. Using the word-processing capabilities of a computer, a minister might start with a sermon outline on the screen and fill it in. Illustrations and main ideas can be listed at random and then later put into order. Blocks of text can be moved from one part of the sermon to another or whole sections can be put aside for possible reconsideration or for use in a future sermon. When asked, the computer can provide information about progress, such as the number of words that have been written. When the sermon is completed, the text can be printed out.

Word processing can also be used to organize and store resources used in preaching and worship. Sermon illustrations can be stored by key word references so that they can be retrieved by the computer. Once illustrations are stored in the computer, it is possible to have the computer create a concordance whenever needed. If a particular phrase is remembered from an illustration, the computer can search through all illustrations for the correct one. Prayers, litanies, calls to worship, and other worship resources can be stored in a computer and recalled as needed.

The examples above illustrate possible computer application in areas where the church is already accomplishing the tasks in other ways. Financial accounts are already being kept, reports prepared, libraries organized, sermons written, mailing lists updated, and sermon illustrations and worship aids filed. In each case the computer is helpful because it provides speed, accuracy, and ease. This speed and accuracy also make it possible to consider using the computer to accomplish some tasks not usually done in churches.

Computers Make New Tasks Possible

Organizing information that is available to the church is the first area where the computer can help accomplish tasks that are too difficult to do manually. A computer can search for information from a variety of sources and then present the information in a usable form. This is particularly useful in identifying target groups for certain church programs.

For example, most churches keep records that would make it possible to discover the names and telephone numbers of all the members who have birthdays in June and are over seventy years old. Finding such information would demand countless hours of searching and comparing lists. If membership information were all stored in a computer, such a list could easily be obtained. If a youth group wanted to have a June birthday party for church members over seventy, for example, the youth could easily obtain the helpful information from a computer.

The possibilities for sorting and organizing the information that churches collect are infinite. For example, membership cultivation programs and financial campaigns could benefit from access to information about patterns of participation and giving.

Secondly, the computer can be used to analyze information. One minister uses a computer to analyze the pattern of visitation in the parish. Each pastoral visit or extended telephone conversation is entered into the computer. This data accumulates over a period of months and can be analyzed by the computer to indicate areas that have been neglected or to show areas where a great deal of time is expended.

The computer can also analyze patterns of participation in church programs or giving and provide information that is usually not available. Without a computer, these tasks are tedious; the benefit of having the information is not great enough to justify the work necessary to obtain it. With a computer, however, the analysis can easily be done and the church benefits from the information.

Finally, the computer can be used to make predictions. A computer could make predictions of expected financial expenditures or predictions on the need for additional space for high-attendance programs. One minister collects data about weather, the seasons, and other variables. The data is combined with church attendance records to make predictions about the makeup of the congregation on upcoming Sundays. This information is then used when plans are being made for the Sunday service. Thus, a sermon about family life would not be planned for a Sunday when the attendance of families with children is expected to be low.

Ministers who own personal computers report that they continue to discover new ways that the computer can help them accomplish tasks. Organization, analysis, and projection are only three areas where the computer can help with new tasks.

Computers and Educational Ministry

Computer-assisted education is in its infancy but already advances in this field can be used in the teaching ministries of the church. In its most primitive form computer-assisted education can be used for learning drills and evaluations. The computer presents information and then presents learning exercises and drills to be used until the material is mastered. For example, computer programs are available that assist in teaching the names of the books of the Bible, thus freeing church school teachers from the task of drilling factual material.

Computer-assisted courses are being taught in some seminaries. The content of the course is put on the computer and the student works at a terminal. The program provides for self-testing: one can evaluate whether the material has been mastered and then focus on unlearned material. These courses could be distributed to ministers or others with personal computers just as television is used to distribute lecture courses from universities.

The computer's ability to organize information and to evaluate it quickly also makes it possible for the computer to aid Christians in individual study. By assisting in the discovery of helpful resources to answer theological and spiritual questions, computers can bring a new dimension to the educational ministry of the church in the near future. For example, a person wanting to look into the subject of spiritual gifts might receive a list of books on the subject from a computer. Or a person could use the computer to search through a particular book for references to a subject of interest. The computer might use a specially prepared index of related theological terms or ideas and search through the tables of contents of books for these terms. Personal computers could be of enormous help in individual study.

Personal Computers as Part of Larger Systems

A personal computer can be part of a telecommunications system. The personal computer serves as a terminal and is connected through telephone lines to other terminals or computer systems. There are several commercial services which provide information from large files of electronically stored data to owners of personal computers. Information about publications, news, sports, and travel are all available. Electronic mail—where messages are sent from one personal computer owner to another—is also available. In the future there may be specialized telecommunication services to aid with ministry.

Computers Are Limited

Any discussion of the possible applications of computers must include a consideration of areas where computers cannot be used.

Much work has been done to develop artificial intelligence in computers. In some ways computers can mimic human activity and even appear to respond as an intelligent human being would respond, but all attempts to create intelligent computers have been unsuccessful. A computer that takes control of its own destiny is still an object of science fiction.

John G. Kemeny in his book *Man and the Computer* suggests that people should develop a mutually supportive relationship with the computer. Looking to the future, he says, ". . . in short, while 99.99 percent of the work will be done by the computer, the 1/100 percent assigned to human beings is an essential contribution to the partnership." The computer, Kemeny adds, cannot decide the best way to use computers. People need to "set the goals and tell the computer how to work toward them." [1]

Claims that computers are accomplishing creative tasks, such as

[1] John G. Kemeny, *Man and the Computer* (New York: Charles Scribner's Sons, 1972), pp. 18-19.

writing novels, might suggest that computers could write sermons. But novels are not actually being written by computers. The computer is assisting in the writing in the same way that a computer might assist with the writing of a sermon by searching through illustrations, biblical material, and commentaries for related phrases or key words—but the computer would only be assisting.

Computers cannot express emotion. This seems obvious, but as the church begins to use computers, it is important to keep in mind the limits of the computer in this area. Computers are already being used for psychological evaluations. The computer evaluates data which indicates the psychological or emotional condition of a person. In this way, also, it can help ministers and other church workers respond in a sensitive way to people. However, any response to a personal problem must be from people and not from a computer. The computer can analyze data that is related to emotion, but it cannot express emotion.

Value judgments may appear to be generated by computers, but the value judgments are actually the result of the information and the instructions that people give the computer. Computers are a tool. The uses to which they are put are determined by the values of the people who choose to use them.

Since many of the people working on computers early in the age of computers were engineers with a primary interest in numbers and mechanical applications, computers often appeared to convert all information into numbers. When computers were used to analyze information about people, the people were assigned numbers. This, however, is not necessary. In situations where value is placed on the names that people have, the computer can use letter symbols or names to stand for a person as easily as it can use a number.

A computer can produce useful information, analysis, or projections only to the extent that it is provided with information and instructions. In turn, the ability of a system to receive and use information is limited by the quality and quantity of equipment that is available. We turn now to this essential examination of computer equipment.

Computer Equipment 3

A computer system is made up of a number of components. These components are sometimes manufactured in a single unit and sometimes they are sold separately. Equipment from several manufacturers can be combined to make a complete system. Printers, disk storage devices, *modems,* and other equipment which can be connected to a personal computer are called *peripheral devices.*

A minimum computer system will consist of an *input* device, a *central processing unit (CPU), memory,* and an *output* device. The input device takes information and converts it into electronic symbols that can be used by the central processing unit. The central processing unit does the computing. The memory stores instructions and data, and the output device converts the results into a form that can be read or understood. One system may have several input devices, a variety of output devices, and several ways that information is stored. Usually there will be only one central processing unit (CPU).

In most cases a computer system for a church or minister will consist of a CPU, a cathode ray tube terminal (CRT) which sends information to the CPU and receives information back, internal memory (to store instructions and data), *floppy disk* storage (used for both instructions and data), and a printer. Each of these is described below with other equipment that might be included in a total system.

Central Processing Unit (CPU)

The "brains" of the computer are found in the CPU. The CPU contains the electronic circuits that make the computer function. People have been building and using CPUs since the early 1950s. What has changed is that today CPUs are small and inexpensive.

The UNIVAC computer, built in 1950, cost several million dollars and filled a large room with electronic equipment. It needed special climate control to insure proper functioning. Today, for about $1,000, you can buy a personal computer that has more computing power than the UNIVAC, is the size of an electric typewriter, and can be used anywhere.

This great reduction in size and cost has been made possible by the development of a technology that places electronic circuits on a piece of silicon. The circuit on a silicon *chip* will have up to twenty-five electronic components in a space the size of the period at the end of this sentence. These circuits are called *integrated circuits*. Computers that use this technology are called microcomputers.

Figure 3—1   A silicon chip that includes the electronic circuits for a 16-bit CPU. (Courtesy of Texas Instruments, Incorporated.)

Most personal computers are designed with a CPU that uses 256 different *machine language* codes for instructions and can use the same number of individual codes for other symbols. These CPUs are called ''8-*bit* CPUs'' because eight on or off signals are used to create the 256 electronic codes. Some computers use a ''16-bit CPU.'' This larger-bit CPU with more instruction codes is faster and can handle more data in a shorter period of time. A 16-bit CPU will not be able to do tasks that are impossible with an 8-bit CPU, but a 16-bit CPU will do tasks faster and more efficiently.

The speed of the CPU, however, will be determined by many factors other than the bit size of the CPU. One factor is the frequency of the internal *clock* of the CPU. Technical descriptions of CPUs will give the frequency in *MHz* units. One MHz is one million counts per second. This means that a clock with 2 MHz would have two million signals per second while a 4 MHz clock would be twice as fast with four million signals per second.

In most cases the design characteristics of the CPU, the quality of software, and the speed of memory and other equipment will be determining factors in establishing how fast a computer will complete a certain job. The only way to know whether a particular CPU is fast enough for your needs is to test it with a specific application, called a *benchmark* program. For example, ask the salesperson to demonstrate how long it takes the computer to alphabetize a list of one hundred names. The best way to know whether a particular CPU will meet your needs is to test it when it is being used with all of the other parts of the system.

CRT Terminal

A CPU requires a terminal of some type so that the operator can input information. A cathode ray tube terminal (CRT) is a typewriter keyboard attached to a screen such as the one a television has. When letters or numbers are typed on the keyboard, they appear on the screen. A "smart" terminal can actually compute or manipulate letters on the screen. A "dumb" terminal cannot do this; it is only an input and output device.

Some computer systems use a regular television screen as a display device. The output from the computer is connected to the antenna terminals of the television using an *RF modulator*. The quality of a television screen limits its use to systems that display forty characters or less per line. Monitors designed for use with computer systems have better resolution and can be used with systems that display a full page of typed material.

The amount of information displayed on the screen may be an important consideration if the computer will be used for word processing. Word processing is possible, nevertheless, with a terminal that will display only thirty-two or forty characters in sixteen rows. It may not be worth the extra cost of the equipment needed to be able to look at a full page on the screen before it is printed. One can quickly learn to visualize how things will look on paper with the information on the screen. When things do not turn out as expected, they can be corrected and the page reprinted.

CRT terminals differ in the set of characters that can be displayed on the screen. Many personal computers print only uppercase letters. Others print both uppercase and lowercase letters. Some CRTs have additional characters. A terminal that displays Greek letters may be particularly useful for ministers. It is possible to overcome some disadvantages of a particular CRT in this area through careful choice of software. For example, a terminal that displays only uppercase letters but provides for the ability to indicate a dark or light background can be *programmed* to show that a letter is uppercase by displaying it automatically with a dark background while lowercase letters have light backgrounds. In this way a less expensive CRT terminal can be used for word processing where it is necessary to see on the screen which letters are uppercase and which are lowercase.

A choice between display in color or black and white is another option in CRT terminals. However, in most church applications a color display will not be necessary.

Internal Memory

Memory is the electronic device that stores the codes for instructions and data. For example, when a computer is used for word processing, the text is stored in the memory of the computer. This means that the more memory there is, the more text the computer is able to store at one time. Personal computers are sold with varying amounts of memory capacity.

Technical specifications will indicate that a computer has from 4 *K* to 64 K *bytes* of memory. A byte is one unit of memory and can be used to store one letter or code. The letter "K" is used to indicate 1,024 bytes of memory space. This means that a 4 K memory has exactly 4,096 bytes—or about 4,000 bytes, to use a round figure. About 3,500 bytes are necessary to store the codes for the letters on one typewritten page. Because the memory space will be used to indicate the organization of the letters and other information, it is better to use the rough estimate that 4,000 to 5,000 bytes will store one page of typewritten material.

Personal computers have two kinds of memories. These are abbreviated "*RAM*" and "*ROM*." Personal computers can have up to 64 K (65,536 bytes) of RAM or ROM memory directly accessible to the CPU.

RAM stands for "random access memory." This memory can be filled with information by the user. It is called random access because the CPU can examine the information stored in any part of this memory directly. The CPU does this by use of a code called *memory address* that indicates where each byte of information is stored in the RAM.

ROM stands for "read only memory." It is also random access in that each byte can be examined in any order but it differs in that its content has been set and cannot be changed by the user. A personal computer will have a certain amount of ROM which contains the instructions to make the computer function properly. This is called the *system monitor*.

The size of the ROM indicates the amount of programming that is built into the computer. However, size of the ROM alone should not be used to compare various computers. The quality and usefulness of the programs in the ROM should be considered. For example, a ROM that contains an elaborate program to control color *graphics* may not be useful in a church setting. The best way to judge the usefulness of the ROM program is to check the ease you have in using the computer.

ROM memory is sometimes supplied in two other forms: *PROM* (Programmable Read Only Memory) and *EPROM* (Erasable Programmable Read Only Memory). These are ROMs that *can* be programmed after manufacture by using a special device.

The content of ROM memory is never lost. When the computer is turned off and on again, the instructions will still be there. RAM memory is much easier to lose; when the computer is turned off, the content of the RAM is lost. This means that RAM can be lost because of power failure.

Memories differ in the speed that they can accept and send out information as well as in other ways. In most cases, these differences will be part of the design of a computer and will have little effect on the usefulness of the computer. One characteristic of RAM that might be important in choosing a computer is whether the memory is *static* or *dynamic*. Static memory has less complicated electronic construction and is dependent only on a constant source of power to insure the accuracy of its content—if the computer is turned on, static memory works. Dynamic memory must receive surges of electricity at specific intervals, or it will fail to retain its information. The necessity for these surges increases the possibility that data will not be accurately stored. Although dynamic memory is much more volatile, it is also less expensive. Therefore, it will be the choice where a well-engineered computer makes it comparable in reliability to static memory.

Because it is impossible to have enough RAM to store all instructions and data used in the computer at one time, another method of storing information is needed in addition to RAM storage. This is called *sec-*

ondary storage. The most common devices used for secondary storage are floppy disks, *hard disks,* and cassette recorders.

Floppy Disks

A floppy disk is a paper-thin plastic disk on which information and instructions are stored. It is covered with a paper envelope and fits into the slot in the front of a *disk drive,* a small box about the size of seven of these books (*Using Personal Computers in the Church*) piled on top of one another. The disk drive is connected to a CPU; in fact, several disk drives can be connected to a CPU so that the information on two or more disks can be used by the computer at once.

Floppy disk drives are designed to use either 8″ or 5¼″ disks. As you would expect, the larger the disk, the more information that can be stored on it. The design of the disk drives, however, also determines the amount of storage space on a disk. Some put the information very close together. Some use one side of the disk. Others use both sides. Most floppy disk systems are designed so that one disk will store at least fifty pages of material.

If a particular application needs to have more information available than can be stored on one floppy disk, there are several possible solutions. One is to have more than one disk drive so that the CPU will have access to the information on more than one disk at a time. A second solution is manually to remove one disk from the disk drive and put another one in. This requires much more human involvement but allows an unlimited amount of information to be available to the CPU because then any number of disks can be used.

The information on the floppy disk is organized so that it can be obtained in any order just as information in RAM is available in any order. However, it takes more time for the CPU to obtain information stored on a floppy disk than to obtain information in internal memory. For most church applications floppy disks will be the best way to store instructions and data.

Hard Disks

Hard disk storage systems will usually not be practical in a church setting. The system operates in essentially the same way but a hard disk drive is four or five times larger than a floppy disk drive. The disk is made of metal and is much more expensive. But hard disks do have certain advantages over floppy disks. Each hard disk will hold about ten times as much information as a floppy disk. Also, it takes only about one-tenth as long to transfer information from the disk to the CPU. Several hard disk drives can be connected to the same CPU so that very large amounts of information are available. Some hard disk systems are designed so that the disk can be removed and another disk placed in the drive.

Cassette Recorder

With most personal computers it is possible to store instructions and data on cassette tapes using an inexpensive tape recorder. This is also an inexpensive way to exchange programs with another personal computer owner. There are several disadvantages. It takes about ten times as long to transfer information from a cassette tape as it takes with a floppy disk and the information is stored sequentially. When information is needed from the cassette, it is necessary to start at the beginning of the tape and look at all the information stored there until the specific information is found. Because cassette recorders were not designed as storage devices for electronic signals, errors will creep into the stored information during the process of transmitting to or transmitting from the recorder or while in storage.

Each computer is designed with a speed at which it will send or receive information. This is called the *baud rate*. The units used are bits per second. If cassette tapes will be the primary method used for storage, then the baud rate of the computer is very important. With a baud rate of 250 bits per second (bps) it will take almost five minutes to store the contents of 64 K of memory on a cassette. However, with a baud rate of 1500 bps, the same amount can be stored in less than a minute.

Printer

Choosing a printer is probably the most difficult part of setting up a computer system. There is a wide range of prices and quality from which to choose. Printers can be divided into two classes: those that produce print with a ribbon and impact it with the shape of the character—called *impact printers*—and those that do not actually hit the paper, which are called *non-impact printers*.

Both the least and the most expensive printers fall into the non-impact printer category. One kind of less expensive printer, the *thermal printer,* uses coated paper which is exposed to heat to copy onto paper the material shown on the terminal screen. Where printed material (*hard copy*) is required but the quality is not important, these inexpensive printers can be used.

In most church applications, the computer will be used for correspondence and other applications where typed pages similar in quality to those produced by an electronic typewriter are needed. This will probably demand an impact printer.

For non-critical tasks where time & money are important, a dot-matrix printer, like the CBM 2022 may be useful. It costs about $800, & prints at about 80 characters per second. It can produce 64 graphics characters, and also ENHANCE characters.

A church might use the 2022 to prepare financial reports & mailing labels, but couldn't fool anyone about the way they were created.

Most churches will need true letter-quality printing. This text was typed with a C. Itoh "Starwriter" printer. It costs $1800. It prints at 25 characters per second, but moves its paper & print head much faster than the CBM 2022 above. Each takes about 3 minutes per page. Note the proportional spacing here, not possible with the CBM printers. True superscripts & subscripts are available, along with some special characters, such as { & }. Also notice the bold face, and underlining.

Figure 3—2   Sample of print using a CBM 2022 and C. Ithol "Starwriter."
(Courtesy of James Strasma.)

Impact printers can be either *solid type printers* or *dot matrix*. Dot matrix letters are those commonly associated with computer printout. Each letter is made up of a group of dots designed from a rectangle of dots: seven dots by nine dots or nine dots by nine dots. Several dot matrix printers are available that produce copy with a quality that compares favorably with solid type printers.

Solid type printers are similar to electric typewriters. A typing element strikes a ribbon that causes a letter to print on the page. The mechanism used on electric typewriters has a maximum speed of fifteen characters per second (*CPS*). Therefore, a *daisy wheel* mechanism has been developed for faster computer printing. A daisy wheel looks like a very small bicycle wheel with a letter at the end of each spoke. The printer rotates the wheel until the proper letter is in position; then a small hammer pushes the letter against the ribbon so that it is printed on the paper. Daisy wheel printers will operate at speeds of up to 55 CPS. This is still slower than dot matrix printers which can produce over 100 CPS.

In some cases a printer can be purchased with the possibility of adding equipment to it when needs change. Some printers are sold with a friction feed system similar to that used on a typewriter. At a future time a pin feed system could be added so that paper with small holes on the edge can be fed into the printer. In most cases, however, the printer cannot be upgraded. Investigate the options carefully before investing in a printer.

If you already own a quality electric typewriter, it may be possible to adapt it as the printer for your computer. In many cases this will provide the most cost-effective way to obtain quality printing.

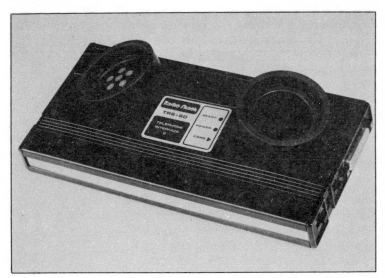

Figure 3—3 An acoustical modem. (Courtesy of Tandy Corporation.)

Modem

"*Modem*¹" is short for *mod*ulator/*dem*odulator. Modems are devices that make it possible for information to be communicated from one computer to another or from a dumb terminal to a distant computer using telephone lines.

There are two types of modems. The first is called "acoustical." These modems have a cradle on which the telephone receiver sits. The device creates sounds and receives sounds. An acoustical modem does not tie up a telephone line or jack except when the computer is using the line. It can be used with any telephone—even a pay phone.

The second type of modem is called "direct-connection modem." These modems plug into a telephone jack and directly create the electronic signal which is carried by the telephone line.

A modem can be either *half duplex* or *full duplex*. Full duplex modems allow information to travel to and from the computer at the same time. Half duplex modems cannot send information while receiving or receive while sending. Some modems will send information more rapidly than others. The baud rate of the modem is the number of bits which will be sent per second.

Other Input/Output Devices

There are many other devices that can be used for input and output of a computer. Some of these are expensive and would probably not have applications in a church. One example would be microfilm readers and printers. These devices are some of the fastest ways to get information into and out of a computer. They have applications where very large amounts of information are being used.

Light pens are very practical. They make it possible to draw on a CRT screen and have the lines feed into the computer. A light pen could also be used to cross off lines of text printed on a screen.

Joy sticks are popular as input devices for computer games. They are small rods which are manipulated to move a spot or other object on the CRT screen.

Devices have been developed that will imitate a human talking or interpret spoken words. These devices involve connecting microphones and speakers to the computer and controlling the input and output with special programs. In this way one can talk rather than use a keyboard to provide the computer with information.

How Does It Work?   4

To use a computer, it is not necessary to understand anything about the way it works, but understanding several very simple concepts will increase your appreciation of the equipment, help you to understand its use better, and help you to evaluate equipment and software.

Computers are electronic devices that convert information into electronic signals, process the electronic signals, and then produce information in a form that can be understood by people. In this they are the same as telephones, tape recorders, telegraphs, and television. But computers do much more than simply return the same information that is given to them. They can analyze, compare, organize, and change information.

Before considering computers, let's take a look at some of the electronic devices that the church and church workers use daily to help with ministry. Telephones take spoken words, change them into electronic signals, and move them over wires to a specific point where the electronic signals are changed back into sound vibrations. Tape recorders will electronically "remember" a pattern that can be recalled and reproduced to sound like the original. If your church uses an electronic answering device, you already use electronics to transfer signals from one place to another and to store them until it is convenient to respond to the information.

A computer carries this one step farther. Not only will the computer store and move information but the computer will also organize, manipulate, and change the information according to a predetermined plan. To understand how it is possible for computers to do this, it is necessary to recognize the distinction between *analog* and *digital* electronic devices.

Figure 4—1   **Computer electronic components. This is an RS-232C interface board for a TRS-80 microcomputer.**
(Courtesy of Tandy Corporation.)

Analog Versus Digital

Electric clocks illustrate the distinction between analog and digital devices. A clock with hands that move in circles in a continuous manner is an analog device. As the hands move smoothly in a circle, they are analogous to the movement of time, and their position indicates the time by analogy. A digital clock is a device which changes time into discrete units and produces numbers to indicate the time. The numbers advance at a specific rate that is the same as the passage of time. A digital clock is designed to divide time into units and report each advance in that unit.

A telephone is an analog electrical device. It takes spoken words and produces an electrical signal which is analogous to sound. If a person speaks more loudly into the telephone, then the strength of the signal slightly increases, and the volume of sound that comes out the other end of the line is also louder.

Telephones were preceded, however, by the telegraph—a digital device. The telegraph transfers information long distances over a wire, but the information must first be translated into Morse code. The code uses the digital principle by representing each letter and number with a series of long and short surges of electricity. A typewriter uses the digital principle as well. It produces a series of distinct characters which represent, rather than are analogous to, spoken words.

Figure 4—2   Codes used in ASCII.

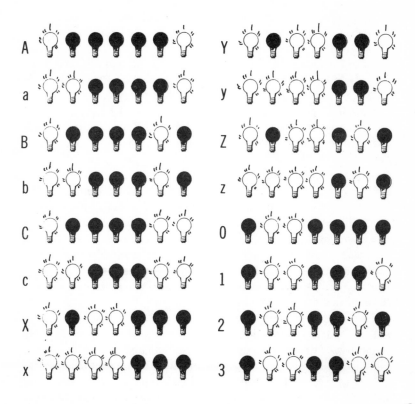

A computer is a digital device. All information used by the computer must first be converted into a code. Written words and numbers are one example of a code. However, computers are not limited to conversions of written words and numbers because scientists have developed ways to translate other information into a digital code. An example of this is a code that stores the pattern of a human voice. This makes it possible for a computer to receive information from a microphone, translate it into a digital code, and later reproduce the sound on a speaker. Computers have also been used to enhance the quality of photographs by converting the patterns of light and dark into a digital code which is analyzed, modified, and returned as a photograph with greater clarity than the original.

Moving and Storing Information

Translating information into an electronic digital form so that it can be used by the computer is the job of input devices. A CRT terminal is the most common input/output device for personal computers.

When a key is pressed on the keyboard, a signal made up of seven units is produced. Each of the seven units is either a strong or a weak surge of electricity. This signal or code can be thought of as if it were seven light bulbs. The bulbs could be on (strong) or off (weak).

Personal computers use a seven-unit code for letters and numbers called *ASCII*. Figure 4-2 shows how the ASCII codes for some letters and numbers could be visualized. The letter "b," for example, has the code of two lights on, followed by three off, followed by one on and one off. A "B" is the same except the second light is turned off rather than on. Using the seven individual units that are either on or off, the input device can produce 128 unique codes. This is sufficient for all the keys on a typewriter plus codes for the space bar and other instructions.

ASCII codes can be carried from the CRT terminal to the computer either on separate wires where each wire will carry one of the units or on a single wire by sending the units one after another with a certain time space between each one. In the first case we say there is a *parallel interface* between the input and the computer. When one wire is used, the computer has a *serial interface*.

The codes from input devices can be transferred very quickly over wires. The rate at which an input device will send messages to a CPU is the baud rate. It will range from one hundred and ten to several thousand codes per second. This method of moving information not only is used to get information from input/output devices to and from the CPU but is also used internally by the computer to manipulate the information.

It would be impossible to store a surge of electricity. Therefore, a different method is needed to save information in memory or temporarily in the CPU. Information is stored by using electronic switches that can be turned either on or off. In memory eight switches are grouped together (such a group is called a byte) to store a specific piece of information. Each individual switch is called a bit.

Information is transferred to and from the CPU over a set of eight wires. An additional sixteen wires are used to send the code for the memory address of the information being sent to or from the CPU. With sixteen wires it is possible to send unique patterns of strong or weak surges of electricity so that 65,536 individual sets of eight memory switches can be addressed.

With ROM (read only memory) the switches have been set either open or closed. In RAM (random access memory) the switches can be turned on or off so that the information they contain can be changed. In either case the computer can check to see what information they contain. When a switch is open, a strong surge of electricity is returned. When a switch is closed, a weak surge is returned.

Figure 4—3 CPU organization.

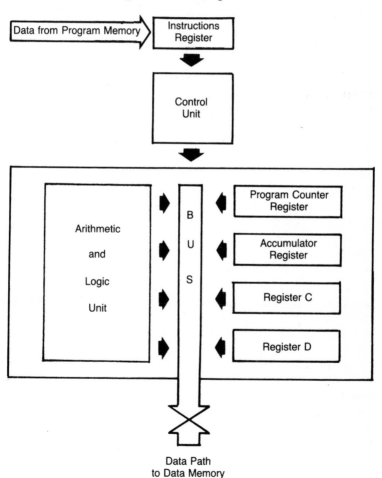

As well as using the memory to store codes for letters and numbers, memory can be used to store codes for instructions for CPU. Instruction codes are made up of eight units. Two hundred and fifty-six unique codes can be made using eight switches that are either open or closed. Each instruction code signals the CPU that a certain set of circuits in the CPU are to be used to move, change, or examine the information which the computer is processing.

CPU Circuits

Information is stored (or remembered) in the CPU using electronic switches—the same way that it is stored in memory. The information is moved in the form of electrical surges from one place to another within the CPU just as it is moved to and from the CPU.

There are three groups of electronic circuits in the CPU. First there is the *control unit* which is a group of electronic circuits that insures that the CPU operates correctly. Secondly, the CPU contains the *registers* which store: (*a*) the information that is being processed, (*b*) the memory address of the next instruction, and (*c*) other information necessary for the computer to function. Thirdly, in the CPU is the *arithmetic and logic unit* containing circuits that, when instructed by the control unit, do logical and arithmetic manipulations on the information stored in the registers.

To understand how the electronic circuits in the CPU function, consider a simple program that would change the codes for a group of letters to make them all uppercase. The set of instructions is written and placed in a certain section of the memory using an input device such as a keyboard. The data to be used is already stored in the memory. Using the keyboard, the address of the first instruction is placed in the *program counter* register. The address of the data also needs to be placed in one of the registers. When all this has been done—the instructions and data have been properly entered into the computer and the registers have been set to the proper initial values—a code is sent to the computer through the keyboard telling it to begin the program.

The computer automatically moves the first instruction from the memory to the control unit. The first instruction tells the control unit that data is to be moved from memory into the *accumulator*. This is accomplished and the program counter advances to the next memory location for another instruction. The second instruction tells the control unit to send the code in the accumulator to a particular circuit in the arithmetic and logic unit where the second switch of the seven switches making up the ASCII code is set open. (This has the effect of making the code uppercase for a letter since all codes for uppercase letters have the second switch open while all codes for lowercase have this switch closed. See figure 4-2.) The control unit calls for the next instruction which sends the uppercase code back to the memory where it is stored. By repeating this series of instructions any number of letters could be quickly changed into uppercase letters. Such a program might be part of a word processing system.

This illustrates the process of writing computer programs in machine language: the computer is given a series of instructions that tell it exactly how to manipulate data. It is possible to program personal computers in machine language. This is seldom done, however, because it is much simpler to give the computer a set of instructions in a language closer to English and have the computer itself translate that language into the codes which will make the computer operate.

To accomplish this task, a computer must have either an *interpreter* or *compiler,* which is a program that translates instructions into machine language code. The interpreter and compiler are computer programs and must be stored in memory. A personal computer has the instructions stored in ROM that are necessary to translate *BASIC* (computer language which uses words rather than codes) into machine language. Writing programs in BASIC is discussed in the following chapter.

The ability to follow a series of instructions is the key to a computer's flexibility and usefulness. Each CPU is designed with a set of circuits capable of manipulating information in a predetermined way. A code tells the CPU which circuit to use. The instructions to the computer do not need to be followed in exactly the same order each time the computer is used. The computer can evaluate data and then, depending on the results, follow one or another set of instructions. Since each individual step is accomplished in a fraction of a second, it is possible for the computer to go through many steps in a short time.

Instructing the Computer 5

The instructions that make a computer accomplish a certain task are called software. This is to distinguish them from computer equipment which is called *hardware*. But the distinction is not always as clear as it might seem. For example, in one computer system the CPU will contain circuits for multiplication. In another system the CPU will be able to do only addition, and multiplication must be accomplished with software that tells the computer to do a series of additions. Two times three becomes two plus two plus two. Both computers will do multiplication, but one uses just hardware and the other uses hardware with software. In either case, the instructions are called the software. All computers need to be guided by software.

Software which is permanently stored in ROM, such as a BASIC interpreter, is sometimes called *firmware* because it is always part of the system and cannot be changed. Personal computers also come with firmware which insures that the computer functions properly. This is called the system monitor.

Where to Get Software

There are three ways to obtain software. You can purchase packages of programs that have been written to meet the needs of many people and are sold for the specific hardware which you own. You can hire someone to write software to meet your specific needs. Or you can write your own software.

In many cases the first option will be the best. There is a great deal of software available. Some of it is very expensive. Other software is almost free or it is in the public domain—that is, it can be used without cost. The cost of a program is not related to its quality.

The only way to know whether particular software will meet your needs is to see it demonstrated or to talk with people who are using the software. Be particularly cautious about software that promises to do too much. Even expensive software with slick advertisements in computer magazines may turn out to be useless for a church application. Software that is specifically written for churches is available from several sources.

Appendix A gives information on several sources of systems and software designed specifically for church use. The list is divided into the categories of suppliers of complete systems and suppliers of software only; complete systems usually include all hardware, software, and support through service contracts. There is some overlap between the two categories, however, because some software suppliers will also help with equipment and some complete systems suppliers also sell custom software.

Some of the best information about software can be obtained from other church people. Talk to someone who is using a computer in a local church and find out what software is being used and what that person has written. Most ministers are willing to share software that they have written for church application. You need to remember that software is covered by the copyright law. It is illegal to make a copy of software which has a copyright notice on it without the permission of the copyright owner.

As well as purchasing programs specifically written for ministers and churches, you will want to obtain some of the software that has been produced for business or personal use. Word processing software is available for most personal computers. This software makes it possible to use a personal computer as a word processor when it is attached to a printer. Mailing list and financial programs are also available. You may find that a data base management program is useful. *VISICALC* is a commercial program that can be used in budgeting and making financial projections.

Software can be purchased by mail or from computer stores. Do not be afraid to test software. A salesperson of quality software will be happy to let you sit at a computer and see how the software works. If it is too complicated for you to understand in the showroom, then it will probably be too complicated for you to use when you have it in your church office.

Also be sure to read carefully the documentation—the written description of applications and use—of the software. Studying the documentation is an excellent precaution against buying unnecessary software. If your mailing list has five hundred names on it, you do not want a mailing list program that will store and sort only two hundred names. Often documentation or software manuals can be purchased separately and studied before the investment in software is made. Also, the cost of the documentation is usually returned if the software is purchased.

Learning to write some of your own software is a surprisingly easy task; all you need to do is learn to write in BASIC. As noted before, personal computers include a BASIC interpreter. The interpreter makes it possible to write software using this *high-level language*.

Software packages for many personal computers can be purchased which make it possible for you to write programs in other high-level languages such as *FORTRAN* (a language commonly used by scientists and engineers), *COBOL* (used for business applications), and *PASCAL* (an all-purpose language useful in writing complicated programs). In most cases, however, BASIC will be sufficient for the programming needs of ministers and church workers.

The best way to learn to program your personal computer in BASIC is to spend three or four sessions using the computer and the manual which comes with the computer. BASIC software which comes with a particular personal computer is similar to, but not exactly the same as, the BASIC provided on computers made by another manufacturer. Programs written in BASIC for one computer will not work on all computers.

It is not possible here to give a complete description of how programs are written in BASIC. The following brief description of BASIC programming illustrates only the principles of programming and shows that anyone can learn to program.

Programming in BASIC

BASIC is called a high-level language. That means that it is composed of English-like sentences that direct the computer. The rules that govern this language must be accurately followed or a program will not work correctly. There are six general types of statements used in BASIC. The types are listed in Figure 5-1 with descriptions of sample statements.

These statements—sometimes called *commands* because they tell the computer what to do—will vary slightly with every computer. Most personal computers will use a BASIC dialect with several more commands than are shown here. There will also be commands to operate the disk system and the printer. The manual which comes with the computer will explain how these commands are used.

Figure 5—1 Examples of statements used in BASIC.

---

1. **input/output**

   10 INPUT y — Waits for an input from the keyboard which ends with carriage return and is assigned a value of y

   20 PRINT x — Causes x to be visible on the CRT

   30 DATA a, b, c — Items a,b,c are the first three pieces of information used when a READ statement appears in a program

   40 READ x — Assigns the next value found in the DATA statements to x

   50 RESTORE — Returns to the beginning of the data list for the next value called for with a READ statement

2. **definitions**

   60 LET x = y — Sets x equal to y

   70 DIM A(x) — Sets the maximum subscript for the variable A as x

   80 REM — Statement is ignored by the computer—provides a way to add lines of explanation or reminders to a program

3. **math and logic functions**

   90 y = ABS(x) — Sets y equal to the absolute value of x

   100 y = SIN(x) — Sets y equal to the sine of x

   110 y = COS(x) — Sets y equal to the cosine of x

   (BASIC also uses conventional signs for addition, subtraction, multiplication, and division, not equal to, greater than, and other math and logic functions)

4. **sequence control**

   120 GOTO n
   130 GOSUB n
   140 RETURN — Advances the program to line number n—program moves to a series of instructions beginning with line n that end in RETURN and program picks up the instruction following line 130

   150   END — The end of program

5. **repeat sequence**

   160 FOR x = a TO b
   STEP z
   170 NEXT x — Begins a loop which ends at NEXT statement. Each time the loop is completed, z is added to x which had an initial value of a. When the value of x reaches b the program moves on to the following 170

6. **choice**

   180 IF x THEN n — If x is a true statement, then the program advances to statement n; if x is not true, the program continues to the next statement.

Imagine that you want to write a program which will sort a list of one hundred names to find people with a particular birthday. Before sitting at the computer to write the program, outline the process necessary to accomplish the task.

You need to:

a) Put one hundred names and birthdates into the computer memory.

b) Tell the computer which date is being searched for.

The computer needs to:

c) Compare the date with each birthday.

d) Print on the CRT the names of people with desired birthday.

After writing the basic outline, prepare a *flowchart*. The symbols used in preparing a flowchart are given in Figure 5-2. The flowchart for our birthday program would look like Figure 5-3.

Figure 5—2 Symbols used in flowcharts.

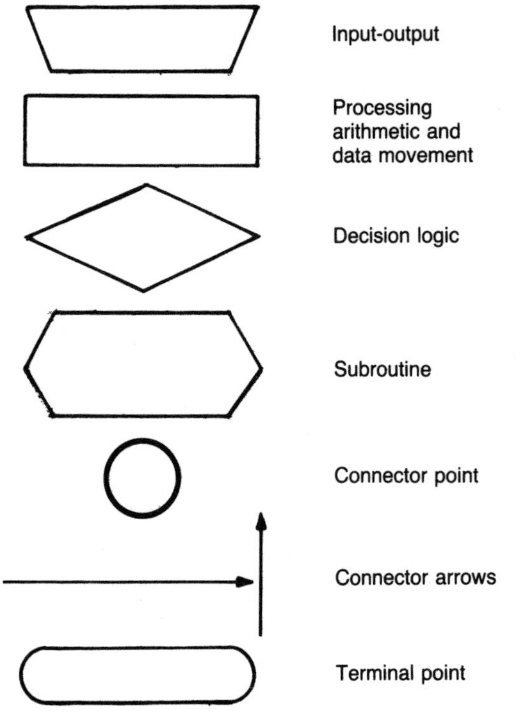

Input-output

Processing arithmetic and data movement

Decision logic

Subroutine

Connector point

Connector arrows

Terminal point

Figure 5-3   Flowchart of birthday program.

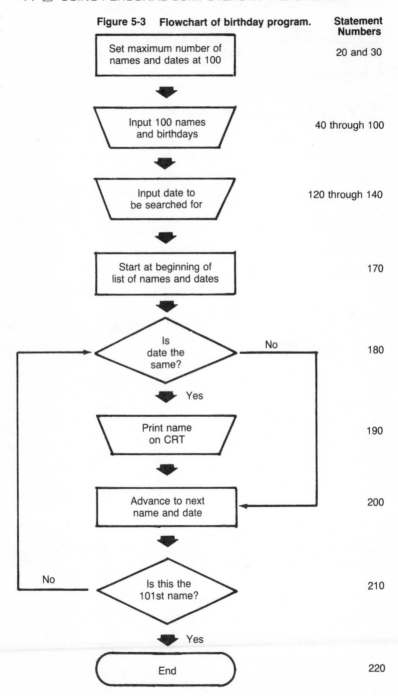

	Statement Numbers
Set maximum number of names and dates at 100	20 and 30
Input 100 names and birthdays	40 through 100
Input date to be searched for	120 through 140
Start at beginning of list of names and dates	170
Is date the same?	180
Print name on CRT	190
Advance to next name and date	200
Is this the 101st name?	210
End	220

Once the flowchart has been written, instructions can be written for the computer. It is best to do this step while sitting at the computer and typing the commands at the keyboard.

Figure 5—4 BASIC listing of birthday program.

```
10  REM    This part of the program enters
             100 names and birthdays.
20  DIM N$(100)
30  DIM BTHDY(100)
40  FOR X = 1 to 100 Step 1
50  PRINT "WHAT IS THE NAME?"
60  INPUT N$(X)
70  PRINT "WHAT IS THE BIRTHDAY?"
80  PRINT "USE NUMBER BETWEEN 1.01 AND 12.31"
90  INPUT BTHDY(X)
100 NEXT X
110 REM    Next the computer asks for a date to search for.
120 PRINT "WHAT DATE DO YOU WANT TO SEARCH FOR?"
130 PRINT "USE NUMBER BETWEEN 1.01 AND 12.31"
140 INPUT DATE
150 REM Each birthday is compared to date.
160 REM When there is a match, the name is printed on the CRT.
170 LET X = 1
180 IF BTHDY(X) ≠ DATE THEN 200
190 PRINT N$(X)
200 LET X = X + 1
210 IF X ≠ 101 THEN 180
220 END
```

When the computer is turned on, a line or square on the CRT indicates where the first character will appear on the screen. This marker is called a *cursor*. Each command begins with a line number or statement number which will determine the order of the steps the computer will later follow. After the command is typed, the carriage return key is pressed. This indicates that the command is completed and another line can be typed. Writing the commands at the computer can save time and frustration because the computer will automatically check each statement to make sure that it is a valid statement in the BASIC language.

In the birthday program birthdates are entered as numbers between 1.01 (January 1) and 12.31 (December 31) so that the computer compares dates as if they were numbers. The number 10.16 would be October 16 while 3.02 would be March 2. Figure 5-4 is a *list* of commands that could be used for a birthday program.

Lines starting with the letters REM will be ignored by the computer. They are written into the program to make the written form of the program easier for you to understand.

Statements 20 and 30 tell the computer that it is necessary to save enough space in memory to store one hundred names and one hundred birthdays. The symbol N$ stands for a name. It is called a *string* variable. The $ indicates that the data is made up of letters rather than numbers. The computer will not attempt to do arithmetic with string variables. BTHDY is the numerical variable. In this program each name will be assigned a particular N$ and each birthday will be assigned a particular BTHDY. Figure 5-5 shows sample values for N$ and BTHDY.

Figure 5—5   Examples of N$s and BTHDYs.

N$(1)	Jane Johnson
BTHDY(1)	3.15
N$(2)	Hosea Castro
BTHDY(2)	12.09
N$(99)	Ron Helms
BTHDY(99)	5.21
N$(100)	Florence Giovanni
BTHDY(100)	1.04

Each of these names and birthdays will be entered into the computer memory with the instructions of statements 40 through 100. This is a FOR...NEXT loop—statement 40 through the series to statement 100—that is repeated one hundred times. The first name and birthdate have the X of 1; the second name and birthdate have the X of 2. The computer will automatically increase the value of X as each successive name is added so that each name and birthday are given a special place in the computer memory.

When all of the names and birthdays have been stored in the computer memory, the CRT will ask for the date which is to be searched for (DATE). This is done with statements 120 through 140.

The last part of the program is written with choice statements rather than a FOR...NEXT loop. It would be possible to write the program with a FOR...NEXT loop, but the choice statement is used to illustrate its function.

Statement 170 tells the computer to begin with the first X; so the computer begins with the BTHDY(1) OF N$(1). If the birthday (BTHDY) is not the same as the date being searched for (DATE), then the program will skip the command to print the name. This is accomplished with statement 180. Statement 190 prints the name of those with birthdays that are the same as DATE. Statement 200 causes the value of X to increase by one. If X has reached 101 (It was at 100 and had 1 added to it), all the names have been checked and the program ends. If X has not reached 101, then the program returns to statement 180 to check the next birthday.

After the program instructions have been typed into the computer, it can be run. This means that the computer proceeds through the steps of the program. To start the program, the word RUN is typed and the carriage return key is pressed.

The computer will go through the steps of setting up a memory area to store the names and birthdays. Then it will print on the screen, "WHAT IS THE NAME?" It will wait for you to type the name and will know the name is complete when you type the carriage return key. The first name will be stored in the first memory area saved for names. When this is done, the computer will print on the screen:

"WHAT IS THE BIRTHDAY?"
"USE NUMBER BETWEEN 1.01 and 12.31."

This number will be stored in the first memory area saved for birthdays. The computer will repeat the same process one hundred times, each time asking for a name and waiting for the name to be typed followed by a carriage return and then doing the same for a birthday. After this has been repeated one hundred times, the computer will print on the screen,

"WHAT DATE DO YOU WANT TO SEARCH FOR?"

When the date has been typed, followed by a carriage return, the computer will proceed to the end of the program and print on the screen the names of people with the birthday asked for, stopping when all one hundred birthdays have been examined.

This simple program illustrates many of the principles of programming but would be refined for actual church use. Names and birthdays would be saved on a disk or cassette for future use. It might also be helpful to clear the screen several times during the program so that it does not become cluttered. The MEMSTAT/BAS program found in Appendix B contains a more sophisticated birthday search program.

How to Get Started 6

S hopping for a computer is as confusing as shopping for a new car. Each manufacturer puts together a package with various characteristics aimed at meeting the needs of the largest number of people in a way that is more attractive than the packages offered by the competition. However, shopping for a computer differs from shopping for a new car in one important way. When needs change, an old car is usually traded for a completely new model. When needs for a computer system change, it is often better to add equipment to the system rather than trading the old system for a new one. This means that the decision about what computer to buy depends on both your present and your future needs.

Shopping for Equipment

The first step in obtaining equipment is to define clearly the need for a computer and to determine exactly how it will be used. Specific information about the size of the job the computer will be asked to do must also be collected. If the computer will be used for mailing lists, it will be necessary to collect information about the mailing lists. How large are they? What information is filed about each person? What will be the intended use for the mailing lists?

Secondly, look at long-term possible uses of the computer. Some capabilities may not be necessary at first but will be very useful in the future. If the computer will be used only for financial records, then a *letter quality printer* is not necessary. Yet if plans for the future might include word processing for church correspondence, a quality printer would be recommended.

Careful evaluation at this stage can avoid problems later. Defining the need for a computer should not be done in a vacuum. Before a commitment is made to purchase hardware, its intended use should be clearly determined.

At one church, for example, parish officials studied their parish and produced an eight-page document with several appendices attached. The study evaluated the time spent by the parish secretary in tasks that could be assisted by a computer, examined ways that a computer could personalize the ministry of the church, and studied the data collected from each household in the church.

Learning about the availability of equipment and software will be part of the choosing process. Remember, it will not matter how sophisticated or advanced your hardware is if you do not have software to make it do what you need. It is dangerous to purchase a computer with the promise that software "will soon be available." The software that is "soon available" may not meet your needs or do all the things that a salesperson says it will.

If you plan on writing your own software, then the characteristics of the BASIC interpreter are very important. Do not just assume that, because a computer has a BASIC interpreter, you will be able to write programs to do all the things you need. The list of available commands should be carefully examined. For example, some forms of BASIC can do arithmetic only with integers.

Once you have identified the computer systems for which software is available that will meet your immediate needs, you still need to consider several other factors. Price is certainly one concern, but there are also other important considerations.

The computer *bus* is one of them. Most computers are designed with electronic circuits attached to a set of wires called the bus. Some computers are designed using a system called the *S-100 bus*. Additional memory, input/output, real time clocks, and other computer devices can be attached to these bus lines. If you purchase a computer with an S-100 bus, it will be possible to add electronic devices from any other manufacturer that uses the same bus.

Apple computers have a unique bus system. Because of the popularity of Apple computers, several manufacturers produce devices which are compatible with the Apple bus. Some computers, however, are designed so that it is not easy to expand them by connecting equipment to the bus lines. The ease with which a computer can be expanded and the availability of hardware compatible with the bus of a particular system should be considered.

Another consideration is the availability of service. Computers will break down and consequently will need to be fixed. Most computers are sold with a guarantee; sometimes an optional service contract is available. It is a good idea to contact people who own hardware similar to whatever you are considering in order to learn about their experience with getting repairs done quickly and well. Computers are most vulnerable to breakdown during the first few months of use. Your warranty, then, is very important.

A last way that shopping for computers is like shopping for an automobile lies in the fact that you will not always need to pay the list price. Careful shopping can result in finding a bargain. Computers are sometimes put on sale, or a used computer might be available to you. You may find that a computer store will give the church a price break because the computer will be in a very visible place with many persons learning how to use it. Purchasing a computer from a mail-order house in a distant state may save several hundred dollars initially but cost much more in the long run if it has to be shipped back for repairs. Again, there are many things to be considered.

When Should You Buy?

Prices of computers will probably go down in the future. It is also likely that the cost of software will go down. The teachers at the Texas Instruments Learning Center predict that the cost of personal computers will decrease by 1985 to one-tenth of the cost in 1980. This prediction should be taken seriously since Texas Instruments has always been aggressive in leading the way with price reductions of computers and parts. Technical advances may result in inexpensive memory and storage devices in the near future.

Computers will also change in design. Predictions are very difficult to make about the development of new technology. Given the technology now available, it seems certain that there will be inexpensive computers that are more powerful and faster than the present models. Purchasing hardware that can easily be added to offers some insurance that equipment will not become obsolete immediately.

Does this mean that you should wait to buy a computer? Probably not. It makes sense to wait only if you cannot afford a computer now. But computers are already bargains. Their potential contribution to the church is much greater than their price tag. If you wait five or ten years to begin using a computer, the work of the church loses the benefit from the use of a computer for those five to ten years. You certainly would not wait five or ten years to buy an automobile to help with church work simply because you hope that more fuel-efficient models will be developed in the future.

Several sample computer systems are described on the following pages. These are systems that might be used by a minister or a church and are available in the early 1980s. Computer design may change and prices are subject to very rapid change. Current manufacturers' specifications should be examined for accuracy of specifications, availability, and prices.

Sample Systems

Radio Shack TRS-80 microcomputers—The Radio Shack TRS-80 microcomputer is the most popular personal computer. It is available at the hundreds of Radio Shack outlets across the country. When it needs to be repaired, it can be returned to the place of purchase, and the outlet will ship it to a repair center. The TRS-80 microcomputer has more software available than any other personal computer. This makes it very attractive.

The popular Model I is no longer available. But you may find a used Model I which will meet your needs.

Model III is available with from 4 K to 48 K of memory. It can be used with disk storage on 5¼″ disks, printers, and telephone modems. All accessories are available from Radio Shack. Printers are available for as little as $219. Radio Shack also sells daisy wheel and quality dot matrix printers.

Model II is Radio Shack's most sophisticated computer. It is designed to be competitive with business computers. The screen will display twenty-four rows of eighty characters which are both uppercase and lowercase.

Model II uses 8″ disks which can store up to half a million characters per disk. BASIC language is not stored in ROM memory area—as it is in Models I and III—but is loaded into the computer's RAM from disk storage each time it is needed. This means that more memory is available for other applications. BASIC is available both with an interpreter and a compiler. Other languages available include *ASSEMBLY*, COBOL, and FORTRAN. Model II is about twice as fast as Model I. A complete Model II system will cost from $4,700 to $9,000.

A TRS-80 microcomputer system that might be used in a church would begin with the Model III computer with 32 K memory installed. This would cost $1,118. Two 5¼″ disk drives can be installed in the computer cabinet. This will cost $1,249. There may be additional charges for the installation of memory and disk drives. The Line Printer IV costs $999 and is a high enough quality dot matrix printer to be used for most word processing needs. It prints both uppercase and lowercase letters at a speed of 50 CPS. Radio Shack sells a word processing software package called *SCRIPSIT/DISK* for $99.95. There are also other word processing software packages available for this system. A mailing list program that will handle up to 990 names costs $99.95. A filing system program that could be used for sermon illustrations or other data costs $99.95. There are also software packages written for the TRS-80 microcomputer available from many other sources. Some have been written specifically for churches. The program listed in Appendix B of this book is a membership program which is part of a package of programs for the TRS-80 microcomputer Model I or III.

Figure 6—1   Radio Shack TRS-80 Model III microcomputer.
(Courtesy of Tandy Corporation.)

A TRS-80 microcomputer Model III system will cost well under $4,000 including all software and extra disks.

One disadvantage of the Radio Shack computers is that the process· of expansion is difficult. If memory is added, the computer must be returned to a service center. Also the features of other models cannot be added; a new model must be purchased. This means that the purchase of a TRS-80 microcomputer must be preceded by very careful planning and consideration of future needs.

Apple II—The Apple II computer is designed for easy expansion as one's needs demand. Expansion does not demand a factory installation. The user simply plugs additional parts into the computer cabinet.

The Apple II is available with 16 K to 48 K bytes of RAM. It also includes 12 K bytes of ROM which contains system control and a BASIC interpreter. The PASCAL language can be added. The Apple II displays twenty-four lines of forty characters each, and an accessory is available that will display eighty characters per line. The Apple II will display only uppercase letters. The word processing program indicates uppercase letters with a dark background and lowercase letters with a light background.

An Apple II computer with 48 K bytes of RAM costs $1,395. Add to that a disk drive for 5¼" floppy disks at $595. The Apple Writer word processing package costs $75. A mailing list software program is $49.95.

Because of the popularity of the Apple II, some software is also available specifically for church applications. Appendix C contains a sample of church software for an Apple II.

The Apple II does not come equipped with a screen. A black and white nine-inch monitor can be purchased from Apple Computers for $240. If you use your own television set, the Apple will produce graphics in color. A Selectric typewriter can be converted for use as a printer for about $500. If you are handy and know a little about electronics, the conversion can be done for much less.

Using a television set and Selectric typewriter which you already have, the total cost of an Apple II system with one disk drive including software is less than $2,700.

PET—The Commodore PET 2001 series has been a very popular computer with computer hobbyists. It is expandable by plugging devices into an expansion bus that is inside the computer case. There is also an IEEE-488 expansion bus which makes it possible to connect disk drives, telephone modems, printers, and other devices which are manufactured according to the IEEE-488 standard.

A PET comes with a screen that displays both uppercase and lowercase letters in twenty-five lines of forty characters. The PET 2001 with 36 K of memory costs about $1,200.

For some church uses Commodore series 8000 will provide the best system. It is based on the PET design but has several improvements. The screen will display eighty characters per line, making it possible to display text in the same format as it will be printed. A dual drive floppy disk stores over 950 K bytes of information. The Commodore 8032, which includes the screen and 36 K internal memory, costs $1,795. The 8050 dual disk drive also costs $1,795.

Software for PET computers is available from Commodore and others. WORD PRO is one of the best word processing programs available for personal computers.

Explorer/85—Building a computer kit can be a rewarding experience for someone with the interest and time. Kits are available from a number of sources. Heathkit sells a computer kit which is very similar to the TRS-80 Model II microcomputer in features (except for a smaller disk capacity) but which costs about half as much. Since you build it yourself, you can also make additions yourself as you decide to expand the system.

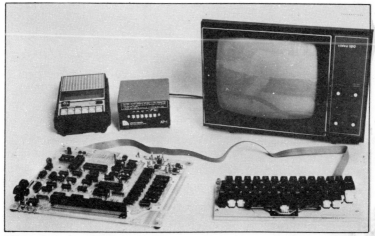

Figure 6—2   Explorer/85 fully expanded.
(Courtesy of Netronics Research and Development Ltd.)

One of the least expensive ways to get started in computers—with a system that can be expanded—is with an Explorer/85 kit. The kit can be purchased in various levels so that expansion is done one step at a time. Level A contains the central processing unit and input/output circuits. It costs less than $130 but needs to be connected to a keyboard/terminal, a television screen, and power supply. A keyboard/terminal kit costs $149. The Level A kit can be assembled in three sessions. The keyboard/terminal kit takes about the same amount of time. Kits include a *printed circuit board* with parts that need to be individually soldered into place. All the parts are guaranteed. For a small fee, the manufacturer will fix an Explorer/85 which has been put together and will not work.

Software for the Level A system must be written in machine language. This is somewhat more complicated than writing programs in BASIC, but the programs are faster and use less memory space. About $200 for additional parts will add 16 K of memory. If you use your own television as a monitor and your own cassette recorder to store programs and data and invest about $500 and the time needed to build the kit and write programs, it is possible to have a computer system useful in any application where hard copy is not necessary.

The system can be expanded by the addition of a printer, additional memory, a floppy disk system (or even hard disks), a BASIC language system, and commercial software including some of the best word processing packages developed for business use. Later additions to the system will not cost you more than they would have if you had not started with a kit.

Computer kits are designed for the person who is interested in computers as a hobby. Without such interest, obtaining a computer by building a kit can result in a great deal of time being spent before producing time-saving or useful applications. Some ministers or other workers in the church will find that building a computer kit is the best way to move the church into the computer age.

Cromemco Z-2H—The same technology that has been developed to make personal computers possible and computer applications cost effective for handling mailing lists of four hundred names can also be applied to much larger systems. In most cases the information available on two or four floppy disks is sufficient for any one use. Disks can be manually changed in the disk drive so that any amount of information can be stored and used by the computer. Yet there may be some situations where it is desirable to have very large amounts of information available at one time or to have access to information at a faster rate than is possible with floppy disks.

The Cromemco Z-2H computer has a central processing unit that is similar to the CPU used in many personal computers. However, this CPU is attached to 64 K of direct memory, two floppy disk drives capable of storing 780 K bytes of programs or information, and a hard disk system which can store eleven million bytes. Several terminals can be attached to this computer. This gives each user access to all of the data and programs. Even when several terminals are in use at the same time, each user has the impression that the computer is completely dedicated to his or her use.

Each terminal will display twenty-four lines of up to eighty uppercase and lowercase characters. Each has a 14-key numeric pad as well and other features, such as a *real time clock* which gives the correct time of day. A high speed Model 3703 dot matrix printer will produce printed material usable for many situations at a rate of 180 CPS. A slower full-letter printer, Model 3355, will print at a rate of only 55 CPS, but produces quality impression suited to camera copy. Software is available from Cromemco and other suppliers. This system could be expanded with additional hard disk storage, terminals, and printers.

The Z-2H computer costs $10,000. Each terminal is $2,000. The Model 3703 dot matrix printer is $3,000, and the letter quality printer is $3,400. This makes the total cost of the equipment described above with three terminals to be about $22,400. The cost for necessary software is very difficult to estimate. The data base management system costs only $100 as does the word processing system. General ledger software costs $1,000. Buying custom software to meet specific needs could cost several thousand dollars. Even so, this complete system that can be used simultaneously by three staff members and print with two printers would still cost well under $30,000.

WS78 by Digital—The Digital Equipment Corporation manufactures computers that are not really personal computers. They are designed for small business and professional offices and offer advantages over the personal computers. A high price is paid for these small advantages; yet in some cases they may be worth the money. Digital sells a service agreement that costs about $100 a month but insures that a malfunctioning computer will be serviced within four hours from the time trouble is reported. It is possible to program the computer using BASIC although there is a large assortment of software available from Digital. Digital stores are found in many cities. These stores sell and service the computers and also offer courses in how to use their equipment.

A computer with a terminal, two disk drives, a letter quality printer, and software packages will cost about $10,000. The word processing system uses a master disk which will store fifty pages of material as well as the word processing program. The second disk will store up to 125 pages of printed material.

Case Studies 7

The nine case studies that follow illustrate the diverse uses of computers in church settings. Some of the church people profiled here are real pioneers not just in church computer work but also in the world of personal computers as a whole. Others are people who have taken little interest in how computers work or in writing programs but have put computer technology to work for the church. All ten persons are enthusiastic about the potential for computer enhancement of ministry.

These case studies are vivid proof that computers offer a vast potential for creative new approaches to ministry. And, as several of the case studies illustrate, the computer can also free church people for more creative and rewarding work.

JIM STRASMA
First United Methodist Church
Post Office Box 647
Pawnee, IL 62558

By the fall of 1978 Reverend Jim Strasma had saved enough money from weddings and funerals to invest in a 795 PET computer with an 8 K memory and a cassette storage system. He began adding equipment and eventually sold his original small computer to pay for a better model with more memory. Today Jim has a Commodore CBM 4032 computer with a 4040 dual disk drive, 2023 dot matrix printer, modem, and a Starwriter letter quality printer. This comes to an investment of about $5,000.

Jim has written many of the programs he uses, including a number that he has sold or traded with other computer programmers. But for many applications he uses commercial programs. WORD-PRO is his favorite word processing program. Jim claims that it is the best available for any personal computer. He also uses the program called VISICALC which allows the user to plan a church budget on the computer and see immediately the effect of possible changes, such as a 25 percent increase in the electric bill. WORD-PRO costs about $350; VISICALC costs $200. Jim uses a database manager and mailing list package called *JINSAM* that keeps track of church visitors. The program package costs over $400, but since Jim is the author of part of the package, he did not need to pay for it.

Jim admits that there is nothing that he does with the computer that could not be done another way, given unlimited time and resources. However, several tasks are done better, faster, and more cheaply with the computer.

Record keeping is one example. With a computer, records can be kept for each member and visitor. All of the following information might be stored in the computer: name, neighborhood, place of employment, attendance habits, a list of small groups within the church of which the person is a member, and a list of times when the minister has visited the person and for what purposes.

Typing tasks are also aided by the computer. Jim prepares his sermons on the computer and gets letter-perfect manuscripts without last minute, hard-to-read corrections. Individualized letters are regularly sent to visitors and other groups. The computer also greatly reduces the work necessary to produce membership rosters, worship bulletins, and Christmas letters.

Jim worries about churches and ministers purchasing bad programs. He suggests that churches purchase the manual first to see whether the program meets specific church needs and look for church programs that link information about family members, update information easily, and have compatibility between the word processing and record keeping programs.

HERBERT MOISE
Beaumont United Presbyterian Church
702 Euclid Avenue
Post Office Box 368
Beaumont, CA 92223

Herbert Moise purchased Kittel's *Theological Dictionary of the New Testament* but found the index difficult to use. He asked a friend who knows about computers whether a computer would help him find entries quickly. After being assured that a computer would make the *Dictionary* more useful, Herb bought a Radio Shack TRS-80 Model I microcomputer. He wrote a program to help him find references in Kittel's *Dictionary* and soon discovered many other uses for the computer. Today Herb no longer uses the index program but is completely sold on the usefulness of the computer in his ministry.

His equipment is a TRS-80 Model I microcomputer which has a 48 K memory and dual disk drive. He has a Radio Shack Model I dot matrix printer. Herb's total investment was less than $3,500.

Herb purchased a set of programs from Exodus Computing. The membership program found in Appendix B is part of that package. The package of programs includes files for biblical references, programs to handle church finances, a calendar and planning program, and several others. Herb uses the membership program each day to check to see which members are having birthdays. He then gives each one a telephone call. Herb purchased the VISICALC program from Radio Shack.

Herb has written a number of other programs himself. He has a program that keeps track of church participation and attendance. After five years of collecting data, Herb can use his computer to identify trends and even make predictions about attendance on a particular Sunday.

He recently began keeping the books for the $200,000 budget of his presbytery. He purchased a packaged financial program and soon saved the presbytery the cost of an expensive CPA. In just a few hours a week Herb can enter all expenditures and incomes. The computer produces a balance sheet and prepares the payroll. The financial information that emerges is obtained quickly and is in a form that is more useful to the presbytery.

Herb has purchased a modem and is looking forward to developing a common data base of sermon material that can be shared with neighboring ministers. He feels that the development of data bases for ministers—with vast amounts of information available—will open exciting new possibilities for ministry.

IAN ROBERTSON
Alhambra Church of the Nazarene
118 North Curtis
Alhambra, CA 91801

In a sense Ian Robertson was forced to consider using a computer system. The demands of responding to mail and raising funds to support a television ministry carried on three hundred cable television stations in thirty-nine states were just too much for non-computer labor. The mailing list of the two-hundred-member Alhambra Church of the Nazarene went from five hundred to five thousand names in six months, and it appeared possible that it would soon reach as high as twenty thousand.

Ian first looked at various computer systems at a computer trade show in Los Angeles and then settled on a Vector Graphic computer sold in nearby Arcadia. The total cost of the computer system including the software was about $8,000. It included a Vector Graphic System B with a CRT. The microcomputer had 65 K RAM internal memory. He also purchased two floppy disk drives, a high speed, letter quality line printer, and a modem.

Word processing, data processing, bookkeeping, and communications software were all purchased as packaged programs. Ian has not written any special programs or purchased any custom software.

Ian initially purchased his computer to sort and process a large mailing list and to merge text with the mailing list to create personalized letters. Several other applications have emerged. He now writes much of the church's sixteen-page magazine himself directly on the Vector terminal using a word processing program. His secretary, Diane Hernandez, edits the copy and puts it into final form on the computer screen. She also selects type styles and sizes and prepares the layout. Rather than carry a copy to the typesetter as she did in the past, Diane places a telephone call to the printer. The computer feeds the newsletter copy over the phone lines where it is set in print by the print shop's computer. This process is not only much faster but also eliminates steps which provide opportunity for error.

The computer has also reduced the time needed to accomplish record keeping tasks. In the past Diane Hernandez would spend three full days each quarter updating and correcting the church school class records. With the assistance of the computer this can now be done in one and a half hours. Preparation of weekly church worship bulletins is also more efficient with the computer, as is church bookkeeping.

As Ian explains, the computer's help with office work has made it possible for the church to provide more ministry. The church secretary has been freed from tedious jobs. She has taken over the youth ministry of the church and even has afternoons when she can leave the office to make visitations to help build the youth programs.

JEFFREY CARLSON
First Presbyterian Church
1111 Fifth Avenue, North
Fort Dodge, IA 50501

Jeffrey purchased a Radio Shack TRS-80 Model I microcomputer with 16 K of memory and a Radio Shack Line Printer II, which is a dot matrix printer. He uses a stringy floppy for storage of data and programs. A stringy floppy uses principles similar to disk storage to store about 60 K of information which appears to the computer to be available as random access off-line storage. This system is much slower than floppy disks but it is also much less expensive.

Jeffrey writes most of his own programs. He has developed a word processing program that he uses for sermon preparation. With his program loaded into the computer, it is possible to write about four double-spaced pages before the text must be saved on his stringy floppy.

He has developed a program to keep track of the details of worship. Hymns, Scriptures, and resources used are recorded so that patterns or large gaps can be discovered.

Jeffrey also uses his computer in premarital counseling. He has developed an inventory which collects information about the couple. The computer analyzes this information and produces a document that can be used as a discussion starter with the couple.

Jeffrey feels that some computer applications are trivial. For example, providing simulation games for youth groups is a nice idea but not worth the investment in computer equipment. However, he is quick to point to ways that his computer contributes to his ministry.

ROGER I. PERKS
Immanuel Presbyterian Church
326 East 156th Street
Cleveland, OH 44110

Roger Perks has had military experience with computers. So it is not surprising that he is benefiting from computer technology at his 150-member church. He uses the services of Cross Computer Service which specializes in providing mailing labels for churches, religious organizations, and mission groups. The address is Box 13026, St. Louis, MO 63119.

Roger sent the church's mailing list of two hundred names to Cross Computer Service. The company charged $16 to have the list entered in their system and then sent back one set of address labels. To change a name on the list costs 8 cents and each set of labels costs $4. The labels come in zip code order. It is also possible to obtain an alphabetical list on plain paper for a small fee.

Roger believes that the production of twelve or fifteen sets of mailing labels each year would not justify his church's investment in a computer system, but his small-membership church can still benefit from computer technology.

RICHARD and JOAN HUNT
Post Office Box 8265
Dallas, TX 75205

Richard and Joan Hunt have designed MIRROR, a Couple Relationship Inventory, to be used with couples either in marriage enrichment or premarital counseling. The booklet, answer sheets, and interpretative guide can be purchased from the Hunts. After a couple completes the answer sheets, their pastor or counselor returns the answer sheets to the Hunts for scoring. The computer-printed profile provides scores on ninety-six scales and other information to aid the couple in understanding themselves and each other better. This profile would be impossible without the aid of the computer.

The Hunts use a Cromemco Z-2 computer with 64 K memory and two disk drives. They also input data with an OpScan 17 optical scanner connected to the Cromemco and have a General Electric 360-line printer for output.

The Hunts are developing computer-assisted instruction materials for couples to use as a supplement to the United Methodist marriage book, *Growing Love in Christian Marriage*. These interactive computer programs can be used on an Apple II or similar microcomputer in a local church setting. The Hunts also score the Theological School Inventory, Inventory of Religious Activities and Interests, and several psychological inventories from Ministry Inventories, a nonprofit service to seminaries and churches.

Dr. Hunt is the chairperson of the North Texas Annual Conference Local Church Software Systems design team. The team is developing software which can be used in any size church of any denomination. The system will include a tutorial function to help new users learn how to operate the system.

Dr. Hunt writes programs in FORTRAN, BASIC, and PASCAL. He is a professor of psychology at Southern Methodist University.

SUE LUTZ
Episcopal Diocese of Washington
Mount Saint Alban
Washington, DC 20016

Sue Lutz's first assignment as an administrative assistant for the Diocese of Washington was to buy a computer system. She had been a parish secretary before coming to the diocesan office and had no experience with office computers. Her husband, a professional in the computer field, helped with the search for a system that would meet the needs of the diocesan office.

Sue examined a large number of systems. Several of the word processing and business computer systems were rejected because they could not be programmed to meet the specific needs of the office. Hobby and personal computers were also rejected because of their limited screen size and the concern that there might be difficulty in obtaining reliable repair service for the computer. (Service contracts were not available for personal computers.) It was decided to purchase a WS 78 manufactured by Digital Equipment Corporation. A letter quality printer was also purchased. The equipment cost $14,000. Within one year the cost of the same equipment dropped about 35 percent, but Sue is still glad that her diocese went ahead and purchased equipment when it did.

Sue says that the computer control of mailing lists has been a major benefit. She keeps a master mailing list with each name coded so that special lists can easily be made. When an address changes, only the master list must be changed. This results in an accuracy that was difficult to achieve before.

She points to the fact that people in the office are now freed for more creative work since documents do not need to be retyped several times. Once written material has been stored on the computer, it can be corrected and reproduced without asking someone to perform the tedious task of retyping.

The ability to produce personalized letters has been a mixed blessing. In the past, information was sent out on photocopied letters addressed to "Dear Friend." With the computer available, office personnel have a tendency to want to personalize every information letter. She says that there are times when a "Dear Friend" letter is acceptable, but people in the office ask for a personalized letter.

With ten years experience as a parish secretary, Sue's only regret is that she didn't have a computer when she worked in a parish.

MONSIGNOR EDMOND CARMODY
Archdiocese of San Antonio
Post Office Box 32648
San Antonio, TX 78284

Monsignor Edmond Carmody is familiar with computers because he has taken fifteen hours of college work in computer science. He originally looked to computer technology to help organize the tribunal docket for the Archdiocese of San Antonio. The one thousand cases handled by the church court are now efficiently monitored by seven people rather than the nine who were needed without the computer.

The archdiocese now uses the computer for much more than processing the tribunal docket and is developing a computer system to help the parishes of the diocese. The sum of $136,000 has been invested in equipment that includes a Texas Instrument DS990 Model 30 with 258 K of memory and a hard disk with 600 *megabytes* of storage space. The archdiocese has both a fast dot matrix printer and a slower, letter quality printer that can produce five hundred letters a day.

Software has been obtained from Membership Services, Inc. All software is provided and maintained for $10,000 per year. The software includes a program to keep track of the tribunal docket, bookkeeping for the archdiocese, word processing, and a program to sort and interpret a census that was taken of 130,000 families. The census program makes it possible to identify people with specific gifts and interests as well as groups that need specialized ministries.

The two hundred parishes of the archdiocese are being encouraged to invest in terminal equipment that can be connected through the phone lines to the central computer. This will make it possible for a parish to update the information in the census and to use it for local planning.

In the future, it is expected that every parish will have a terminal where contributions and expenses will be entered into the central computer. The terminal will also be used for word processing. Each parish will have an inexpensive dot matrix printer and possibly a high quality printer which will be used to print financial information, membership reports, and other written material. Because some equipment will be shared by many parishes, an individual parish will need to invest very little to be able to benefit from a full range of computer services.

Monsignor Carmody sees the coming of computers as a wonderful tool for ministry. Computers, he says, make it possible to personalize communication.

HAL R. STOCKERT
Saints Peter and Paul's Byzantine Catholic Church
2 Park Avenue
Granville, NY 12832
(for SOURCE subscribers use, SOURCE Number TCD #139)

Hal was "forced" to learn something about computers when in the late 1960s he was working on a degree in business administration.

The degree program required introduction courses in COBOL and FORTRAN programming languages. He began doing some home study and, when Radio Shack introduced computers, he bought one for himself. Today he has the TRS-80 Model I microcomputer's two disk unit and a Line Printer II. He also has a modem so that he can be connected to SOURCE which is a commerical time-sharing system and information data base (The address for SOURCE is 1616 Anderson Road, McLean, VA 22102). Hal has invested about $4,000 in equipment and software which includes SCRIPSIT/DISK, VISICALC, MICROFILES, GENERAL LEDGER and MAILING LIST.

He has also written some software which he uses to keep track of contributions and to prepare quarterly statements for members of the parish. Hal does all the bookkeeping for a parish which includes 177 adults. With the computer it takes several afternoons a month rather than two days every week to take care of all the record keeping and related chores.

Hal has also found that the computer opens up possibilities for ministry to young people. He has built a youth club around computerized games.

As one of the first customers of SOURCE, Hal has had experience with computer communications and information retrieval. It is in this area that Hal sees some of the greatest potential for use of computers by the church.

Hal is working to convince his diocese that parishes should be linked by computer communications to the chancery office. This would make it possible to share programs and data and increase parish and diocese efficiency. Hal sees many possibilities: central record keeping, central data registry, and the sharing of scientific analysis of trends within individual parishes. Hal envisions a day when problems could be anticipated using sketchy data rather than waiting until the problem is full blown to deal with it.

The Future 8

Because the use of computers depends on the creative genius of those who design computers and develop their applications, it is difficult to predict what the future uses of computer technology will be. In the near future the great advances will not be made in the development of a completely new technology but rather in the application of what is already possible and already happening in some places. Because we can anticipate changes in hardware, data bases, and software, each will be discussed briefly.

Hardware Changes

Sixteen-bit central processing units for personal computers are already available. The 16-bit CPU has more machine language instructions so that programs can be executed more quickly. In the near future 32-bit CPUs will be available for personal computers. They will be even faster, have more instruction codes, and handle more data.

Bubble memory is already available. As it becomes less expensive, it will provide large amounts of information storage that can be accessed directly and will not be destroyed when the computer is turned off. We can expect bubble memory components with a surface area of one square inch that will store 128 K bytes of information.

Because *video disk* players store information in a digital form, they can be adapted to store input for a computer system. One video disk has enough space to store a whole encyclopedia. Rather than printing reference books on paper, reference material could be stored on video disks. You could direct the computer to search for the desired information and then read the information on the screen or have it printed out. Large libraries of computer programs could also be distributed on video disks.

Flat screens will replace cathode ray tubes for computer output. The flat screens take up less space, use less energy, and are easier to read without causing eye fatigue.

The church office of the not too distant future might have a flat screen terminal for both the minister and the church secretary. Each terminal would have a powerful 32-bit CPU with 256 K bytes of bubble memory. A bank of bubble memory with two million bytes to store data collected in the parish would be shared, as would a video disk system with software and reference material: telephone books, dictionaries, commentaries, and other data. A letter quality printer would produce all hard copy. When a problem needing information not available on the video disk or in the memory bank is encountered, the computer would automatically dial a telephone number and be connected to a computer system where the information could be obtained.

Central Data Base

Already there are extensive data bases available to anyone with a computer terminal. In the future more information of interest to ministers and church workers will be put on large data bases which will be accessed through a computer terminal. A large *host computer* with a capacity to store large amounts of information will serve as a center of this *network*. But communications between terminals in the network will also be possible.

All continuing education opportunities, for example, will be centrally indexed and information about them available from a data base. The computer could be asked to list all the opportunities to learn about counseling people with alcohol problems that will be offered during the next six months within three hundred miles of a particular city. Reservations could be made in the same way airlines use computers for reservations.

Services such as the Library of Congress search service will be expanded. As indexes of religious literature become computerized, it will be possible to do sophisticated literature searches from a minister's study. In some cases the text of articles will be sent directly to a computer terminal. In other cases microfiche or other hard copy of the material will be obtained after the search.

Today most printed material passes through a stage where it is recorded as a series of electronic signals. These electronic signals are used to set type. In the future it will not be necessary to put these electronic signals into type because they can be distributed directly to computer terminals or stored electronically in libraries for future reference.

Access to data bases will provide not only direct information but also data which can be used in combination with locally collected information. Census data can be combined with statistics about a particular congregation to identify target groups for whom the church will want to develop programs.

Localized data bases will also be developed. A group of ministers in a community might have a common data base of sermon resources around the lectionary texts. Each minister could contribute illustrations and resources to the common file. These could be accessed by all and used for worship preparation. Shared data bases might be set up by a denomination in a geographical region to keep track of members who move within that area and make sure they are contacted by a new church. A data base of hospital patients could be used to insure that all members are visited even when there are many hospitals in an area.

Denominational offices could establish computerized data bases of membership and other statistics. By sending statistics directly to the denominational office through a computer, several steps which can create error can be eliminated.

Software

In the very near future software will be available for all the basic needs of churches. Word processing software is already well developed. Financial software is also available as are a large number of programs for membership and mailing list control. These will improve as they become more specific and will be able to be tailored for specific denominations.

However, we can expect that much more sophisticated software will become available: software that can be used as a diagnostic tool in church programming or planning as well as counseling, software that will produce reliable and useful projections, software to facilitate the management of time and other resources of ministry.

Computers will also be used in the continuing education of ministers and the teaching ministry of the church. Already computer-assisted education programs have been developed for seminarians in areas ranging from introduction to Greek to human sexuality. The computers can provide information and also test mastery of information or provide learning drills. Computers will be as revolutionary as cassette recorders in providing a way for ministers to learn or improve skills.

Computers will be used to teach children and adults the basics of the

Christian faith and to allow interaction for learning about oneself and God in a deeper way. One can imagine a church library which would store disks to be borrowed so that people can take them home and, with their own computers, study a topic—for example, the relationships among the synoptic gospels and a comparison of their contents.

Computers and Christianity

Just as the invention of the printing press affected the practice of ministry, making it possible for every individual Christian to possess a Bible, so the computer may radically change ministry and even the way Christian piety is practiced.

Before the printing press the Scriptures were possessed only by the clergy and a few others. The reading and study of the Scriptures were limited to a small percentage of all Christians. Scriptures were most often used in a worship setting. Today most Christians have a copy of the Bible and many own several other religious books. But for the most part only the clergy have large libraries that include commentaries and reference books about the Bible as well as books about Christian history and theology. The content of Christian scholarship is presented during a sermon at worship by the clergy who are possessors of the books and the training which make it possible for clergy to prepare sermons.

The computer age opens the possibility that all of the information which has been used by the clergy can become readily available to every Christian. Large computer data banks will make word searches in books about theology possible for everyone. It will be possible for every Christian to own not only a Bible but also several video disk recordings of libraries of religious information. So, for example, a person could sit down at home with a computer with a video disk machine and have the computer search through a video disk of sermons to discover what preachers have said about the topic of the virgin birth. Or the computer could search for references and allusions to a certain passage of Scripture to discover interpretations that have been proposed.

Christians have always had access to the presence and power of the Holy Spirit. The printing press made it possible for every Christian to have direct access to the resource of the Scriptures. The computer will make it possible for Christians to have easier access to the resources of the Christian tradition.

Appendix A
Sources of Software and Complete Systems for Church Use

Software

1. PET computer owners will find that **Christian Computer/Based Communications, 44 Delma Drive, Toronto, Canada M8W 4N6** is an invaluable source of information about programs for PET computers.

2. **Church Resource System (CRS), Post Office Box 990, Dallas, TX 75221** supplies software for churches which is designed for use on several personal computers. CRS can also help churches obtain hardware from Radio Shack stores by supplying discount coupons.

3. **Cross Educational Software, Post Office Box 1536, Ruston, LA 71270** sells several Christian education programs for Apple II computers.

4. **Custom Data, Post Office Box 1066, Alamogordo, NM 88310** sells a software package called CHURCH DONATIONS. The package includes nine programs designed for small- to medium-sized congregations. It is designed for either TRS-80 Model I or Model II microcomputers with two disk drives and an eighty-column line printer.

5. **ERB Software, Post Office Box 58713, Houston, TX 77258** has developed a software package which was tested at the Clear Lake United Methodist Church in Texas. It is designed for the Radio Shack TRS-80 Model II microcomputer. The package includes programs for worship, membership, stewardship, and finance data collection and analysis.

6. **Exodus Computing, 1326-A Seventh Avenue, Honolulu, HI 96816** is a source of software for churches with Radio Shack TRS-80 Model I or III microcomputers. The membership programs in Appendix B are part of a total church package called EFFICIENT PASTOR'S STUDY.

7. **G.R.A.P.E., Post Office Box 283, Port Orchard, WA 98366** is a church program exchange organization for owners of Apple com-

puters. Inexpensive software is supplied on disks. The mailing list program in Appendix C is a sample of a program distributed by G.R.A.P.E.

Complete Systems

1. **Church Growth Data Services, 150 South Los Robles Avenue, Suite 600, Pasadena, CA 91101** (800-423-4844) markets two systems: Insight 2000 and Insight 1000. Insight 2000 is for the church with two thousand or more members. It is a complete church computer package using a CMS-1 computer with hard disk storage and any number of terminals and printers. Insight 1000 is for a church with five hundred to three thousand members. It is a complete system using a Vector Graphics computer with hard disk storage.

2. **Church Systems Inc., 3005 South Ponderosa Plaza, Oklahoma City, OK 73115** sells a complete computer system using Data Point equipment. The software includes 230 programs and is designed for a growth-oriented church.

3. Another company which has developed a complete system using Data Point equipment is **Data Management Consultants, Inc., 119 Seventeenth Avenue South, Nashville, TN 37203.**

4. **Membership Services, Incorporated, Post Office Box 2130, Irving, TX 75061** produces custom software and also has a software package for churches called INCHURCH 80. The INCHURCH 80 system is designed to use a Texas Instruments DS990 Model 4 with a Texas Instruments Model 810 dot matrix printer and a Qume daisy wheel letter quality printer. This system uses 911 Texas Instruments terminals.

5. **Video Dynamics, Inc., Post Office Box 20330, Jackson, MS 39209** has developed a complete computer system for a church using the IBM System/23 Datamaster computer.

Appendix B
MEMBER/BAS and MEMSTAT/BAS

MEMBER/BAS and MEMSTAT/BAS are programs written in BASIC for a TRS-80 Model I micromputer with TRS-80 DOS version 3.2, 32 K bytes of RAM, and two disk drives. The two programs are part of a total package of programs for ministers which includes the following programs:

- a Scripture-related reference library
- an annual calendar of daily reminders
- a periodic annual budget analysis
- a church membership visitation data entry and inquiry
- a library cross reference index system.

MEMBER/BAS is a church membership data entry program. It establishes the data base which is used with both the MEMSTAT/BAS and another program to keep track of pastoral visits called CALLING/BAS.

The programs will work if only partial information is known about individuals but it is possible to enter data on each person in all of the following categories:

Name
Membership I.D
Address
Zip
Residence Phone Number
Office Phone Number
First Church Office
Second Church Office
Third Church Office
Occupation
Marital Status
Birthday
Remarks

"Membership I.D." is a code for the category of membership. The program is written with categories used in the United Methodist Church. For use with different membership categories, Lines 16, 17, and 46 need to be modified.

MEMSTAT/BAS is a member data management program that sorts the information available from the MEMBER/BAS program. When the program is used, there are ten options:

Birthday
Age Display
Membership Distribution
Alphabetical Listing
Name(s) by Age
Name(s) by Membership
Name/Address by Zip
Name(s) by Church Office
Bad Birthdates
To Exit Program

Most of the options have obvious applications. With birthday, for example, a date is given to the computer, and it finds all the people with that specific birthday. If no one is found to have a birthday on that day, the following day is searched and so on until a birthday is found. Then the computer prints the name and birthday. Name/Address by Zip prepares a list for address labels. Bad Birthdates produces a list of those people for which no birthday is entered in the data file.

MEMBER/BAS and MEMSTAT/BAS have been written by Thomas M. Moore, CDP, and Reverend Theodore R. Lesnett of Exodus Computing, 1326-A Seventh Avenue, Honolulu, HI 96816. These programs are part of a software package called EFFICIENT PASTOR'S STUDY. It is available as a listing which must be typed into the computer or on a disk which can be used immediately.

Purchase of this book constitutes license for single personal use of MEMBER/BAS and MEMSTAT/BAS. Distribution of these programs is prohibited. Information about modification, use, and availability of these programs as well as information about the complete software package should be obtained from the authors, Moore and Lesnett.

Figure B—1   MEMBER/BAS and MEMSTAT/BAS listings.

```
1 '***MEMBER/BAS***   (C) COPYRIGHT EXODU
S COMPUTING 1980,81
2 CLS: CLEAR513: OPEN"O",2,"MEMBER": PRI
NT#2,0: CLOSE#2
3 CLEAR
4 CLS: PRINT: PRINT"M E M B E R / B A S"
: PRINT: PRINT"OPTIONS:": PRINT: PRINT"1
.  ADD NEW RECORD","2.   DELETE OLD RECOR
D": PRINT: PRINT"3.   CHANGE OLD RECORD",
"4.  VIDEO DISPLAY BY NAME": PRINT
5 PRINT"5.  NOMINATIONS CLEAR","6.  EXIT
 PROGRAM": PRINT: INPUT"OPTION # ";O: IF
 O<1 OR O>7 THEN 4
6 ON O GOTO 11   ,36   ,41   ,81   ,8
 ,96
7 GOTO3
8 OPEN"R",1,"MEMBER/DTA": E=LOF(1): IF E
=0 THEN 9    ELSE 10
9 CLOSE#1: KILL"MEMBER/DTA": GOTO1
10 FIELD1, 110 AS A$, 9 AS B$: FORX=1TOE
: GET1,X: C$="----------": D$=A$: LSETA$=
D$: LSETB$=C$: PUT1,X: NEXTX: CLOSE#1: G
OTO3
11 OPEN"R",1,"MEMBER/DTA": E=LOF(1): FIE
LD 1, 33 AS N$, 2 AS J$, 50 AS S$, 5 AS
Z$, 10 AS T1$, 10 AS T2$, 3 AS C$, 3 AS
C1$, 3 AS C2$, 37 AS O$, 1 AS M$, 8 AS B
$, 63 AS R$: OPEN"I",2,"MEMBER": INPUT#2
,P7: CLOSE#2: IFP7=1THEN14
12 FORX=1TOE: GET1,X: IF"EMPTY"=LEFT$(N$
,5)THEN15
13 NEXTX: OPEN"O",2,"MEMBER": PRINT#2,1:
 CLOSE#2
14 X=E+1
15 GOSUB95   : LINEINPUT"NAME(LAST NAME
FIRST): ";N1$
16 GOSUB95   : PRINT:PRINT"FM = FULL MEM
BER": PRINT"PM = PREPARATORY MEMBER": PR
INT"AF = AFFILIATE MEMBER": PRINT"AM = A
SSOCIATE MEMBER (ANOTHER DENOMINATION)":
```

```
PRINT"CM = CONSTITUTIENT MEMBER": PRINT
"FR = FAMILY RELATIONSHIP": PRINT
17 INPUT"MEMBERSHIP I.D. (FM,PM,AM,AF,CM
,FR) ";J1$: IFJ1$<>"FM"ANDJ1$<>"PM"ANDJ1
$<>"AM"ANDJ1$<>"AF"ANDJ1$<>"CM"ANDJ1$<>"
FR"THEN18    ELSE19
18 PRINT: PRINT"ILLEGAL CODE -- REENTER
CODE": FOR R3=1TO800: NEXT R3: GOTO 16
19 GOSUB95    : PRINT"ADDRESS (STREET (LE
AVE TWO BLANK SPACES) CITY,STATE):":LINE
INPUTS1$: GOSUB95    : INPUT"ZIP: ";Z1$:
GOSUB95
20 INPUT"RESIDENCE PHONE # ";T3$: IF LEN
(T3$)>10 THEN 20
21 GOSUB95
22 INPUT"OFFICE PHONE # ";T4$: IF LEN(T4
$)>10 THEN 22
23 GOSUB95    : INPUT"1ST CHURCH OFFICE "
;C3$: INPUT"2ND CHURCH OFFICE ";C4$: INP
UT"3RD CHURCH OFFICE ";C5$: GOSUB95    :
LINEINPUT"OCCUPATION ";O1$: GOSUB95    :
INPUT"MARITAL STATUS ";M1$: GOSUB95
24 PRINT"BIRTHDATE (MM/DD/YY):": INPUT"(
IF NONE ENTER 'NONE') ";B1$: IF B1$="NO
NE" THEN 34
25 G4=LEN(B1$): IF G4<>8 THEN 29
26 IF MID$(B1$,3,1)<>"/" THEN 29
27 IF MID$(B1$,6,1)<>"/" THEN 29
28 GOTO 31
29 PRINT
30 PRINT"ILLEGAL DATA! ---  REENTER DATE
":GOTO24
31 IF VAL(LEFT$(B1$,2))<1 OR VAL(LEFT$(B
1$,2))>12 THEN 30
32 IF VAL(MID$(B1$,4,2))<1 OR VAL(MID$(B
1$,4,2))>31 THEN 30
33 IF VAL(RIGHT$(B1$,2))<0 THEN 30
34 GOSUB95    : LINEINPUT"REMARKS: ";R1$
35 LSETJ$=J1$: LSETN$=N1$: LSETS$=S1$: L
SETZ$=Z1$: LSETT1$=T3$: LSETT2$=T4$: LSE
TC$=C3$: LSETC1$=C4$: LSETC2$=C5$: LSETO
$=O1$: LSETM$=M1$: LSETB$=B1$: LSETR$=R1
```

```
$: PUT1,X: CLOSE#1: GOTO3
36 INPUT"NAME TO DELETE: ";N1$: L=LEN(N1
$): OPEN"R",1,"MEMBER/DTA": FIELD1, 33 A
S N$, 222 AS N9$: E=LOF(1): FORX=1TOE: G
ET1,X: IFLEFT$(N$,L)=N1$THEN39    ELSE37
37 NEXTX: PRINT: PRINTN1$;" NOT FOUND!
(CHECK SPELLING?)": FOR Q5=1TO600: NEXT
Q5
38 CLOSE#1: GOTO3
39 PRINT: PRINTN$;N9$: PRINT: PRINT"CORR
ECT REFERENCE TO DELETE (Y/N=ENTER)";: I
NPUTY3$: IF Y3$<>"Y"THEN38
40 FIELD1, 5 AS N$, 250 AS N1$: LSETN$="
EMPTY": LSETN1$="": PUT1,X: CLOSE#1: GOT
O3
41 PRINT: LINEINPUT"NAME TO CHANGE:   ";N
$: L=LEN(N$): OPEN"R",1,"MEMBER/DTA": FI
ELD 1, 33 AS N1$: E=LOF(1): FORX=1TOE: G
ET1,X: IFLEFT$(N1$,L)=N$THEN43
42 NEXTX: PRINT: PRINTN$;" NOT FOUND (CH
ECK SPELLING?)": FORN8=1TO750: NEXTN8: C
LOSE#1: GOTO3
43 FIELD1, 33 AS N$, 2 AS J$, 50 AS S$,
5 AS Z$, 10 AS T1$, 10 AS T2$, 3 AS C$,
3 AS C1$, 3 AS C2$, 37 AS O$, 1 AS M$, 8
 AS B$, 63 AS R$: GET1,X: CLS: PRINTN$:
INPUT"CHANGE NAME (Y/N=ENTER)";V$: IFV$=
"Y"THEN44    ELSE45
44 INPUTV1$: LSETN$=V1$: V1$="": V$=""
45 CLS: PRINTJ$: INPUT"CHANGE MEMBERSHIP
 STATUS (Y/N=ENTER)";V$: IFV$="Y"THEN46
   ELSE50
46 INPUTV1$: IF V1$<>"FM"ANDV1$<>"PM"AND
V1$<>"AM"ANDV1$<>"AF"ANDV1$<>"CM"ANDV1$<
>"FR"THEN48    ELSE49
47 LSETJ$=V1$
48 PRINT: PRINT"ILLEGAL CODE -- REENTER
CODE": FOR R3=1 TO 800: NEXT R3: GOTO 46
49 LSETJ$=V1$: V1$="": V$=""
50 CLS: PRINTS$: INPUT"CHANGE ADDRESS (Y
/N=ENTER)";V$: IFV$="Y"THEN51    ELSE52
```

```
51 LINEINPUTV1$: LSETS$=V1$: V1$="": V$=
" "
52 CLS: PRINTZ$: INPUT"CHANGE ZIP (Y/N=E
NTER)";V$: IFV$="Y"THEN53    ELSE54
53 INPUTV1$: LSETZ$=V1$: V1$="": V$=""
54 CLS: PRINTT1$: INPUT"CHANGE RESIDENCE
 PHONE (Y/N=ENTER)";V$: IFV$="Y"THEN55
 ELSE57
55 INPUTV1$: IF LEN(V1$)>10 THEN 55
56 LSETT1$=V1$: V1$="": V$=""
57 CLS: PRINTT2$: INPUT"CHANGE OFFICE PH
ONE (Y/N=ENTER)";V$: IFV$="Y"THEN58    EL
SE60
58 INPUTV1$: IF LEN(V1$)>10 THEN 58
59 LSETT2$=V1$: V1$="": V$=""
60 CLS: PRINTC$,C1$,C2$: INPUT"CHANGE CH
URCH OFFICES (Y/N=ENTER)";V$: IFV$="Y"TH
EN61    ELSE62
61 INPUT"1ST ";V1$: LSETC$=V1$: V1$="":
INPUT"2ND ";V1$: LSETC1$=V1$: V1$="": IN
PUT"3RD ";V1$: LSETC2$=V1$: V1$="": V$="
"
62 CLS: PRINTO$: INPUT"CHANGE OCCUPATION
 (Y/N=ENTER)";V$: IFV$="Y"THEN63    ELSE6
4
63 LINEINPUTV1$: LSETO$=V1$: V1$="":V$="
"
64 CLS: PRINT;M$: INPUT"CHANGE MARITAL S
TATUS (Y/N=ENTER)";V$: IFV$="Y"THEN65
ELSE66
65 INPUTV1$: LSETM$=V1$: V1$="": V$=""
66 CLS: PRINTB$: INPUT"CHANGE BIRTHDATE
(Y/N=ENTER)";V$: IFV$="Y"THEN67    ELSE77
67 INPUT"MM/DD/YY (IF NONE ENTER 'NONE')
";V1$: IF V1$="NONE" THEN 76
68 G4=LEN(V1$): IFG4<>8THEN72
69 IFMID$(V1$,3,1)<>"/"THEN72
70 IFMID$(V1$,6,1)<>"/"THEN72
71 GOTO 73
72 PRINT: PRINT"ILLEGAL DATA!  ---  REEN
TER DATE": FORYB=1TO700:NEXTYB:GOTO66
73 IF VAL(LEFT$(V1$,2))<1 OR VAL(LEFT$(V
```

```
1$,2))>12 THEN 72
74 IF VAL(MID$(V1$,4,2))<1 OR VAL(MID$(V
1$,4,2))>31 THEN 72
75 IF VAL(RIGHT$(V1$,2))<0 THEN 72
76 LSETB$=V1$: V1$="": V$=""
77 CLS: PRINTR$: INPUT"CHANGE REMARKS (Y
/N=ENTER)";V$
78 IFV$="Y"THEN79    ELSE80
79 LINEINPUTV1$: LSETR$=V1$: V1$="": V$=
""
80 PUT1,X: CLOSE#1: GOTO3
81 INPUT"NAME ";N1$: L=LEN(N1$): OPEN"R"
,1,"MEMBER/DTA": FIELD1, 33 AS N$, 2 AS
J$, 50 AS S$, 5 AS Z$, 10 AS T1$, 10 AS
T2$, 3 AS C$, 3 AS C1$, 3 AS C2$, 37 AS
O$, 1 AS M$, 8 AS B$, 63 AS R$, 2 AS L$,
 2 AS L1$, 2 AS L2$: E=LOF(1)
82 FORX=1TOE: GET1,X: IFLEFT$(N$,L)=N1$T
HEN84    ELSE83
83 NEXT X: PRINT: PRINTN1$;" NOT FOUND (
CHECK SPELLING?)": FORD4=1TO670: NEXTD4:
 CLOSE#1: FORH=1TO600: NEXTH: GOTO3
84 CLS: PRINT: PRINTN$;"MARITAL=";M$;"
";"BIRTHDAY: ";B$: PRINTS$;" ZIP:";Z$: P
RINT: PRINT"PHONES: RESIDENCE: ";T1$;" O
FFICE: ";T2$: PRINT: PRINT"CHURCH OFFICE
 CODES: ";C$;" ";C1$;" ";C2$;"    MEMBERS
HIP STATUS: * ";J$;" *": PRINT
85 PRINT"OCCUPATION: ";O$: PRINT: IF VAL
(L$+L1$)<1THEN86    ELSE87
86 PRINT"LAST PASTORAL VISITATION:  !! N
ONE RECORDED !!": GOTO88
87 PRINT"LAST PASTORAL VISITATION: ";L$;
"/";L1$;"/";L2$
88 GOTO89
89 CLOSE#1: PRINT: PRINT"PRESS (C) TO CO
NTINUE"
90 V$=INKEY$: IF V$="C"THEN3
91 IFV$="R"THEN93
92 GOTO90
93 PRINT@704,CHR$(31);: PRINT"REMARKS:"
94 PRINTR$: GOTO89
```

```
95 CLS: PRINTTAB(15)"*** ADD NEW RECORD
SECTION ***": PRINT: RETURN
96 CLS: CLOSE#1: END
```

```
1 '***MEMSTAT/BAS*** (C) COPYRIGHT EXOD
US COMPUTING 1980,81
2 OPEN"R",1,"MEMBER/DTA": IF LOF(1)<1 TH
EN 3     ELSE 4
3 CLOSE#1: KILL"MEMBER/DTA": CLS: PRINT"
DATA FILE 'MEMBER/DTA' IS NOT ON DISK--U
SE 'MEMBER/BAS' FIRST!!": END
4 CLOSE#1
5 CLEAR 514: CLS'***MEMSTAT/BAS***
6 CLS: PRINT: PRINT"M E M B E R S H I P
/ B A S": PRINT: PRINT: PRINT"1.   BIRTHD
AY",,"2.   AGE DISPLAY": PRINT: PRINT"3.
  MEMBERSHIP DISTRIBUTION","4.   ALPHABETI
CAL LISTING": PRINT: PRINT"5.   NAME(S) B
Y AGE","6.   NAME(S) BY MEMBERSHIP"
7 PRINT: PRINT"7.   NAME/ADDRESS BY ZIP",
"8.   NAME(S) BY CHURCH OFFICE": PRINT: P
RINT"9.   BAD BIRTHDATES","10.   TO EXIT P
ROGRAM": CLEAR: PRINT: INPUT"OPTION # ";
P1: IF P1<1 OR P1>10 THEN 5
8 ON P1GOTO9    ,31  ,75  ,86  ,105
,136 ,146 ,165 ,178 ,177
9 OPEN"R",1,"MEMBER/DTA": FIELD1, 33 AS
N$, 124 AS A$, 2 AS M$, 1 AS D1$, 2 AS D
$, 1 AS D4$, 2 AS Y1$: CLS: PRINT: INPUT
"TODAY'S MONTH (MM)";M1$: PRINT: INPUT"T
ODAY'S DAY (DD)";D2$: PRINT: INPUT"TODAY
'S YEAR (YY)";Y2$: PRINT
10 IF VAL(M1$)<1 OR VAL(M1$)>12 OR VAL(D
2$)<1 OR VAL(D2$)>31 THEN 11   ELSE12
11 CLS: PRINT: PRINT"ENTERED DATE IS ILL
EGAL!!": FORX=1TO750: NEXTX: GOTO9
12 E=LOF(1): CLS: PRINT: PRINT"SEARCH DA
TE MONTH ";M1$;" DAY ";D2$: FORX=1TOE:
GET1,X: IF VAL(M1$)=VAL(M$)ANDVAL(D2$)=V
AL(D$)THEN20
```

```
13 NEXT X: IFH7=0THEN15    ELSE14
14 CLOSE#1: LINEINPUT"PRESS (ENTER) KEY
TO CONTINUE";K$: GOTO6
15 A7=VAL(D2$): IFA7=>31THEN17
16 A7=A7+1: D2$=STR$(A7): D2$=RIGHT$(D2$
,2): GOTO12
17 A7=1: A8=VAL(M1$): IFA8=12THEN18    EL
SE19
18 A8=1: D2$=STR$(A7): M1$=STR$(A8): D2$
=RIGHT$(D2$,2): M1$=RIGHT$(M1$,2): GOTO1
2
19 A8=A8+1: D2$=STR$(A7): M1$=STR$(A8):
D2$=RIGHT$(D2$,2): M1$=RIGHT$(M1$,2): GO
TO12
20 IFH7=1THEN22
21 PRINT"THE FOLLOWING PERSON(S) HAVE BI
RTHDAYS TODAY ";: H7=1: PRINT
22 IFVAL(M1$)<VAL(M$)THEN23    ELSE 24
23 Y=(VAL(Y2$)-VAL(Y1$))-1: GOTO 27
24 IFVAL(M1$)>VAL(M$)THEN25    ELSE26
25 Y=VAL(Y2$)-VAL(Y1$): GOTO27
26 IFVAL(D2$)<VAL(D$)THEN23    ELSE25
27 IF Y<0 THEN 29
28 PRINTN$;"    AGE: ";Y:Y=0:PRINTMID$(A$,
3,55):GOTO30
29 PRINTN$:PRINTMID$(A$,3,55)
30 GOTO13
31 CLS: OPEN"R",1,"MEMBER/DTA": FIELD1,
157 AS D2$, 2 AS M$, 1 AS D1$, 2 AS D$,
1 AS D3$, 2 AS Y$: PRINT: PRINT"ENTER CU
RRENT DATE:": PRINT: INPUT"TODAY'S MONTH
  (MM)";M1$: INPUT"TODAY'S DAY    (DD)";
D4$: INPUT"TODAY'S YEAR    (YY)";Y1$
32 IF VAL(M1$)<1ORVAL(M1$)>12ORVAL(D4$)<
1ORVAL(D4$)>31ORVAL(Y1$)>1000RVAL(Y1$)<1
THEN33    ELSE34
33 CLS: PRINT: PRINT"ENTERED DATE IS ILL
EGAL!!": FORX=1TO750: NEXTX: CLOSE#1: GO
TO31
34 IFX9=1THEN35    ELSE36
35 CLS: PRINT"USE SHIFT KEY AND @ KEY TO
STOP SCROLLING OF NAMES": PRINT
```

```
36 E=LOF(1): FORX=1TOE: GET1,X: IFVAL(M$
)=0ORVAL(D$)=0ORVAL(Y$)=0THEN37      ELSE39
37 T=T+1
38 NEXTX: CLOSE#1: GOTO55
39 IFVAL(M1$)<VAL(M$)THEN40       ELSE41
40 Y=(VAL(Y1$)-VAL(Y$))-1: GOTO44
41 IFVAL(M1$)>VAL(M$)THEN42       ELSE43
42 Y=VAL(Y1$)-VAL(Y$): GOTO44
43 IFVAL(D4$)<VAL(D$)THEN40       ELSE42
44 IF Y<0 THEN33
45 IFX9=1THEN111
46 IFY>0ANDY<5THENT1=T1+1
47 IFY>4ANDY<14THENT2=T2+1
48 IFY>13ANDY<18THENT3=T3+1
49 IFY>17ANDY<26THENT4=T4+1
50 IFY>25ANDY<40THENT5=T5+1
51 IFY>39ANDY<56THENT6=T6+1
52 IFY>55ANDY<65THENT7=T7+1
53 IFY>65THENT8=T8+1
54 T9=T9+1: Y=0: GOTO38
55 IFX9=1GOTO134
56 CLS: PRINT: IF T9<1 THEN 57      ELSE 58
57 CLS: PRINT: PRINT"INVALID SAMPLE.    TH
ERE IS NO ONE (1) VALID BIRTHDAY.": FORG
6=1TO900: NEXTG6: GOTO1
58 PRINT"           AGE DISTRIBUTION GRAP
H": PRINTTAB(10)"0%";TAB(34)"16%";TAB(59
)"33.3%": PRINT"0-4";TAB(10): L=INT(150*
(T1/T9)): IF L<1GOTO60
59 FORG=1TOL: PRINT"*";: NEXTG
60 PRINTT1;"(";: Z=INT(1000*(T1/T9))/10:
 PRINTZ;"%)": PRINT"5-13";TAB(10): L=INT
(150*(T2/T9)): IF L<1GOTO62
61 FORG=1TOL: PRINT"*";: NEXTG
62 PRINTT2;"(";: Z=INT(1000*(T2/T9))/10:
 PRINTZ;"%)": PRINT"14-17";TAB(10): L=IN
T(150*(T3/T9)): IF L<1GOTO64
63 FORG=1TOL: PRINT"*";: NEXTG
64 PRINTT3;"(";: Z=INT(1000*(T3/T9))/10:
 PRINTZ;"%)": PRINT"18-25";TAB(10): L=IN
T(150*(T4/T9)): IF L<1GOTO66
65 FORG=1TOL: PRINT"*";: NEXTG
```

```
66 PRINTT4;"(";: Z=INT(1000*(T4/T9))/10:
   PRINTZ;"%)": PRINT"26-39";TAB(10): L=IN
T(150*(T5/T9)): IF L<1THEN68
67 FORG=1TOL: PRINT"*";: NEXTG
68 PRINTT5;"(";: Z=INT(1000*(T5/T9))/10:
   PRINTZ;"%)": PRINT"40-55";TAB(10): L=IN
T(150*(T6/T9)): IF L<1THEN70
69 FORG=1TOL: PRINT"*";: NEXTG
70 PRINTT6;"(";: Z=INT(1000*(T6/T9))/10:
   PRINTZ;"%)": PRINT"56-64";TAB(10): L=IN
T(150*(T7/T9)): IF L<1THEN72
71 FORG=1TOL: PRINT"*";: NEXTG
72 PRINTT7;"(";: Z=INT(1000*(T7/T9))/10:
   PRINTZ;"%)": PRINT"65 +";TAB(10): L=INT
(150*(T8/T9)): IF L<1 THEN 74
73 FORG=1TOL: PRINT"*";: NEXTG
74 PRINTT8;"(";: Z=INT(1000*(T8/T9))/10:
   PRINTZ;"%)": PRINT: PRINT"TOTAL MEMBERS
   COUNTED ";(T+T9);"   TOTAL VALID BIRTHDA
TES ";T9: PRINT: LINEINPUT"PRESS (ENTER)
KEY TO CONTINUE";K$: GOTO6
75 OPEN"R",1,"MEMBER/DTA": FIELD 1,33 AS
   N$, 2 AS S$: E=LOF(1): FOR X=1TOE: GET1
,X: IF W2=1THEN141
76 IF S$="FM" T1=T1+1
77 IFS$="PM"T2=T2+1
78 IFS$="AF"T3=T3+1
79 IFS$="CM"T4=T4+1
80 IFS$="FR"T5=T5+1
81 IFS$="AM"T7=T7+1
82 NEXTX: CLOSE#1: IFW2=1THEN145
83 CLS: PRINT: PRINT"MEMBERSHIP DISTRIBU
TION CHART": PRINT: PRINT"FULL MEMBERS";
TAB(40)"TOTAL=";T1;" OR ";: PRINT INT(10
0*T1/E);"%": PRINT: PRINT"PREPATORY MEMB
ERS";TAB(40)"TOTAL=";T2;" OR ";: PRINTIN
T(100*T2/E);"%": PRINT
84 PRINT"AFFILIATE MEMBERS";TAB(40)"TOTA
L=";T3;" OR ";: PRINTINT(100*T3/E);"%":
PRINT: PRINT"ASSOCIATE MEMBERS";TAB(40)"
TOTAL=";T7;" OR ";: PRINTINT(100*T7/E);"
%": PRINT: PRINT"CONSTITUTE MEMBERS";TAB
```

```
(40)"TOTAL=";T4;" OR ";
85 PRINTINT(100*T4/E);"%": PRINT: PRINT"
FAMILY RELATIVES";TAB(40)"TOTAL=";T5;" O
R ";: PRINTINT(100*T5/E);"%": PRINT: LIN
EINPUT"PRESS (ENTER) KEY TO CONTINUE";K$
: GOTO6
86 CLEAR9000: CLS: PRINT: PRINT"NAMES WI
LL APPEAR IN ALPHABETICAL ORDER:": PRINT
: OPEN"R",1,"MEMBER/DTA": FIELD 1, 33 AS
 N$: E=LOF(1): IF E=1 THEN 87    ELSE 88
87 GET 1: PRINT"1.   ";N$: CLOSE#1: GOTO
102
88 DIMR$(E): FORX=1TOE: GET1:IFLEFT$(N$,
5%)="EMPTY"THEN90
89 E4=E4+1:R$(E4)=N$
90 NEXTX: CLOSE#1:E=E4
91 FORX=1TOE: A$=R$(X): A=X: IFA$="["GOT
O100
92 FORY=XTOE: IFA$<R$(Y)THEN94    ELSE93
93 A$=R$(Y): A=Y
94 NEXTY: IFX8=1THEN95    ELSE96
95 PRINTA$:R$(A)="[": GOTO91
96 V=V+1: IF X9=1 GOTO 99
97 IF W2=1 GOTO 99
98 PRINTV;".   ";A$
99 R$(A)="[": GOTO91
100 NEXTX: IF X9=1 AND X8=0 THEN 101   EL
SE 102
101 PRINT: PRINT"THERE ARE NO PERSONS BE
TWEEN ";I2;" AND ";M;" AGES": PRINT: GOT
O 104
102 IF W2=1 AND R=0 THEN 103   ELSE 104
103 PRINT: PRINT"THERE ARE NO PERSONS WI
TH REQUESTED MEMBERSHIP DESIGNATION"
104 LINEINPUT"PRESS (ENTER) KEY TO CONTI
NUE";K$: GOTO6
105 CLEAR9000: CLS: PRINT@192,"ENTER MIN
IMUM AGE ";: INPUTA: I2=A: INPUT"ENTER M
AXIMUM AGE ";M: IF A>M THEN 107   ELSE106
106 IF A<0 OR M>110 THEN 108   ELSE 110
107 CLS: PRINT: PRINT"HOW CAN ";A;" BE A
```

```
  MINIMUM AGE WHEN ";M;" IS LESS???": GOT
O 109
108 CLS: PRINT: PRINT"ILLEGAL:MINIMUM AG
E LESS THAN Ø OR MAXIMUM AGE GREATER THA
N 110"
109 FORX=1TO999: NEXTX: GOTO105
110 X9=1: GOTO31
111 IFY=>A AND Y<=MTHEN113
112 GOTO38
113 IF X8=1THEN115
114 DIMR$(E): X8=1
115 IF Y=1THEN116  ELSE117
116 R=R+1: R$(R)="  1"+"   "+LEFT$(D2$,33
): GOTO38
117 IFY=2THEN118  ELSE119
118 R=R+1: R$(R)="  2"+"   "+LEFT$(D2$,33
): GOTO38
119 IFY=3THEN120  ELSE121
120 R=R+1: R$(R)="  3"+"   "+LEFT$(D2$,33
): GOTO38
121 IFY=4THEN122  ELSE123
122 R=R+1: R$(R)="  4"+"   "+LEFT$(D2$,33
): GOTO38
123 IFY=5THEN124  ELSE125
124 R=R+1: R$(R)="  5"+"   "+LEFT$(D2$,33
): GOTO38
125 IFY=6THEN126  ELSE127
126 R=R+1: R$(R)="  6"+"   "+LEFT$(D2$,33
): GOTO38
127 IFY=7THEN128  ELSE129
128 R=R+1: R$(R)="  7"+"   "+LEFT$(D2$,33
): GOTO38
129 IFY=8THEN130  ELSE131
130 R=R+1: R$(R)="  8"+"   "+LEFT$(D2$,33
): GOTO38
131 IFY=9THEN132  ELSE133
132 R=R+1: R$(R)="  9"+"   "+LEFT$(D2$,33
): GOTO38
133 R=R+1: R$(R)=STR$(Y)+"   "+LEFT$(D2$,
33): GOTO38
134 E=R: GOTO91
```

```
135 INPUT"PRESS (ENTER) KEY TO CONTINUE"
;K: GOTO6
136 CLEAR9000
137 CLS: PRINT@192,"MEMBERSHIP DESIGNATI
ONS:": PRINT: PRINT"FULL MEMBERSHIP.....
..... FM": PRINT"PREPATORY MEMBERSHIP...
.. PM": PRINT"AFFILIATE MEMBERSHIP.....
AF": PRINT"ASSOCIATE MEMBERSHIP..... AM"
: PRINT"CONSTITUENT MEMBERSHIP... CM"
138 PRINT"FAMILY RELATION.......... FR":
 PRINT: PRINT"ENTER MEMBERSHIP DESIGNATI
ON DESIRED: ";: INPUTL7$: IF L7$="FM" OR
 L7$="PM" OR L7$="AF" OR L7$="AM" OR L7$
="CM" OR L7$="FR" THEN 140  ELSE 139
139 PRINT: PRINT"ILLEGAL ENTRY  --  REEN
TER MEMBERSHIP DESIGNATION!": FOR B7=1TO
700: NEXTB7: GOTO 137
140 W2=1: GOTO75
141 IFS$=L7$THEN142  ELSE82
142 IFX8=1THEN144
143 DIMR$(E): X8=1
144 R=R+1: R$(R)=N$: GOTO82
145 E=R: GOTO91
146 CLS: CLEAR9000: OPEN"R",1,"MEMBER/DT
A": E=LOF(1): IF E=1 THEN 147  ELSE 148
147 FIELD 1, 33 AS N$, 2 AS J$, 50 AS S$
, 5 AS Z$: CLOSE#1: PRINT"1.   ";N$: PRIN
TS$: PRINTZ$: PRINT: GOTO 161
148 FIELD 1, 33 AS N$, 2 AS J$, 50 AS S$
, 5 AS Z$: DIMZ1$(E): DIMZ3$(E): DIMZ4(E
): PRINT@450,"RETRIEVING DATA": FORX=1TO
E: GET1,X: IFVAL(Z$)<1THEN150
149 Z1$(X)=Z$: Z4(X)=X: GOTO151
150 T$="00000": Z1$(X)=T$: Z4(X)=X
151 NEXTX: CLS: PRINT@450,"PROCESSING ZI
P CODES:": PRINTZ1$(1): Z3$(1)=Z1$(1): Z
3=Z3+1: FORX=2TOE: FORY=1TOZ3: IFZ1$(X)=
Z3$(Y)THEN155
152 NEXTY: GOTO154
153 GOTO155
154 Z3=Z3+1: Z3$(Z3)=Z1$(X): PRINTZ3$(Z3
): GOTO155
```

```
155 NEXTX: CLS: PRINT@450,"NOW ORGANIZIN
G ZIP CODES:"
156 FORX=1TOZ3-1: IFZ3$(X)>Z3$(X+1)THEN1
58
157 NEXTX: CLS: PRINT: PRINT"NAME, ADDRE
SS BY ZIP:": PRINT: PRINT: GOTO159
158 Z6$=Z3$(X): Z3$(X)=Z3$(X+1): Z3$(X+1
)=Z6$: GOTO156
159 FORX=1TOZ3: FORY=1TOE: IFZ3$(X)=Z1$(
Y)THEN162  ELSE160
160 NEXTY: NEXTX: CLOSE#1
161 LINEINPUT"PRESS (ENTER) KEY TO CONTI
NUE";K$: GOTO6
162 GET1,Z4(Y): IFLEFT$(N$,5)="EMPTY"THE
N160
163 I=INSTR(N$," "): N1$=RIGHT$(N$,33-I)
: I2=INSTR(N1$," "): PRINTLEFT$(N1$,I2)
;" ";: PRINTLEFT$(N$,I): I=INSTR(S$,"  "
): PRINTLEFT$(S$,I+1): S1$=RIGHT$(S$,50-
(I+1)): I3=INSTR(S1$,"  "): PRINTLEFT$(
S1$,I3+4);: PRINTZ$: Z1$(Y)="0": PRINT
164 GOTO160
165 OPEN"R",1,"MEMBER/DTA": FIELD 1, 33
AS N$, 77 AS B$, 3 AS C$, 3 AS C1$, 3 AS
 C2$: CLS: PRINT"   ***NAMES BY CHURCH O
FFICE CODE***": PRINT
166 LINEINPUT"PLEASE ENTER A THREE (3) C
HARACTER CODE: ";A$: A9=LEN(A$): IF A9<>
3 THEN PRINT"CHARACTER CODE MUST BE THRE
E (3) IN LENGTH!"
167 IFA9<>3THEN166
168 E=LOF(1): FORX=1TOE: GET1,X: IF A$="
---"THEN169  ELSE171
169 IFC$=A$ANDC1$=A$ANDC2$=A$THEN173
170 GOTO 175
171 IFC$=A$ORC1$=A$ORC2$=A$THEN173
172 GOTO175
173 PRINTN$: C=C+1: IFC>13THEN174  ELSE1
75
174 PRINT: PRINT"PLEASE PRESS (ENTER) KE
Y FOR MORE NAMES";: LINEINPUTY$: C=0: GO
TO175
```

```
175 NEXTX: CLOSE#1: PRINT: IF C=0 PRINT"
THERE ARE NO MEMBERS WITH REQUESTED CHUR
CH OFFICE"
176 PRINT: PRINT"PRESS (ENTER) KEY TO CO
NTINUE";: LINEINPUTQ2$: GOTO6
177 CLS: END
178 CLS: CLEAR514: PRINT: PRINT"RESEARCH
ING MEMBER FILE FOR NAMES WITHOUT VALID
BIRTHDATE": PRINT: OPEN"R",1,"MEMBER/DTA
": FIELD1,33ASN$,124ASD2$,2ASM$,1ASD1$,2
ASD$,1ASD3$,2ASY$: E=LOF(1): FORX=1TOE:
GET1,X: IF"EMPTY"=LEFT$(N$,5)THEN184
179 IFVAL(M$)=0ORVAL(D$)=0ORVAL(Y$)=0THE
N180  ELSE184
180 I=INSTR(N$," "): IF I=0 THEN 181  EL
SE182
181 PRINTN$,M$;"/";D$;"/";Y$: GOTO 183
182 I1=INSTR(I+1,N$," "): N1$=MID$(N$,1,
(I1-1)): PRINTN1$;"  ";M$;D$;Y$
183 T=T+1
184 NEXTX: CLOSE#1: PRINT"TOTAL=";T: PRI
NT: PRINT"PRESS (ENTER) KEY TO CONTINUE"
;: LINEINPUTDE$: GOTO6
```

Appendix C
Addresses Plus

ADDRESSES PLUS is written in Applesoft BASIC. It is written for use with an Apple II computer with disk drive and a printer. The program assumes that the printer interface card is in Slot 1 of the Apple II computer. If you have placed the printer interface card in another slot, then Line 120 must be modified by changing the value of SLOT.

Each entry has an Identification number, two name lines, two address lines, city, state, zip, a quantity, and a comment. The quantity can be any number. It could be used to record attendance or contributions or anything else that can have a numerical value. The comment line could be used to store a reminder—for instance, a record of the last pastoral visit or any other comment about the person. The program will sort the list according to identification numbers, names, cities, states, or zip codes. These lists can be examined and changed on the CRT or printed on 1-inch or 1-1/2-inch address labels.

This program has been written by Steven Lawson, the founder of G.R.A.P.E. (Group for Religious Apple Programming Exchange). The program along with several other useful programs is supplied by G.R.A.P.E. on a disk.

Steve Lawson, Post Office Box 283, Port Orchard, WA 98366 should be contacted directly with questions concerning use of this program. Purchase of this book constitutes a license for single personal use of this program. For information about the G.R.A.P.E. policy on wider distribution of this program, write to Steve Lawson.

Figure C—1   ADDRESSES PLUS listing.

```
10  HOME : VTAB 3: PRINT  TAB( 7)"*** ADDRESSES PLUS  ***"
    : PRINT : PRINT  TAB( 9)"BY STEPHEN M. LAWSON": VTAB 1
    0: PRINT  TAB( 9)"DISTRIBUTED 1980 BY:": PRINT : PRINT
    TAB( 9)"THE G.R.A.P.E. PRESS": VTAB 16
20  LL = 6: PRINT "ADDRESSES IN DISK FILE ARE EITHER DIS-": PRINT
    "PLAYED OR PRINTED.  ONE INCH LABELS ARE": PRINT "STAN
    DARD.": PRINT
30  INPUT "  DO YOU WISH TO USE 1 1/2 INCH LABELS?";A$: PRINT
    : IF  LEFT$ (A$,1) = "Y" THEN LL = 9
40  REM
*** READ DATA ***

50  NO = 50: DIM NA$(NO,9),R(NO),SRT$(NO):D$ =  CHR$ (4)
60  ONERR  GOTO 100: PRINT D$"OPEN ADD.LIST"
70  PRINT D$"READ ADD.LIST"
80  FOR J = 1 TO NO: FOR I = 1 TO 9
90  INPUT NA$(J,I):R(J) = J: NEXT : NEXT
100  POKE 216,0:NO = J - 1: PRINT D$"CLOSE"
110  REM
*** INITIALIZE ***

120  BLANK = 0:FIND = 0:CHOICE = 0:LN = 0:ST = 1:ND = NO:COP
     IES = 0:SLOT = 1:I = 0:J = 0:K = 0:L = 0
130  REM
*** SELECTION ***

140  HOME : PRINT "** THE G.R.A.P.E. ADDRESS LIST **": PRINT
     : PRINT : PRINT "INDICATE CHOICE:   ";:TB = PO * 5 + 1

150  IF  NOT PO THEN  PRINT  TAB( 20)"PRINTER IS OFF": GOTO
     170
160  PRINT  TAB( 20)"PRINTER IS ";: FLASH : PRINT "ON": NORMAL

170  PRINT : PRINT "                      0 LIST ALL": PRINT : PRINT
     "                    1 BY NUMBER": PRINT : PRINT "
              2 BY RECORD"
180  PRINT : PRINT "                      3 BY STATE": PRINT : PRINT
     "                  4 PRINTER ON/OFF": PRINT : PRINT "
                 5 SORT RECORDS": PRINT : PRINT "
              6 CHANGE/END"
```

```
190 PRINT : INPUT "        CHOICE: ";A$:CHOICE = VAL (A$
    ): IF CHOICE = - 1 THEN 210
200 PRINT : ON CHOICE GOTO 410,540,520,530,570: IF CHOICE THEN
    830
210 IF CHOICE = - 1 THEN PO = 0: CALL 1013: GOTO 120: REM
    RE-ACTIVATES UC/LC OPTION IFUSED - USE WITH CAUTION!!
    !!
220 REM
*** MAIN PROGRAM ***

230 HOME : IF PO THEN PRINT CHR$ (4)"PR#"SLOT
240 FOR K = 1 TO COPIES: FOR J = ST TO ND:I = R(J): ON FIN
    D GOTO 250,270: GOTO 280
250 IF ID = VAL (NA$(I,1)) THEN 280
260 GOTO 380
270 IF LEFT$ (NA$(I,7),2) < > ST$ THEN 380
280 IF NOT PO THEN PRINT J, VAL (NA$(I,1))
290 PRINT TAB( TB);NA$(I,2): IF NA$(I,3) < > "" THEN PRINT
    TAB( TB);NA$(I,3):LN = LN + 1
300 PRINT TAB( TB);NA$(I,4): IF NA$(I,5) < > "" THEN PRINT
    TAB( TB);NA$(I,5):LN = LN + 1
310 PRINT TAB( TB);NA$(I,6): PRINT TAB( TB);NA$(I,7):LN =
    LN + 4: IF PO THEN 360
320 IF NA$(I,8) < > "" OR NA$(I,9) < > "" THEN PRINT
330 IF NA$(I,8) < > "" THEN PRINT "QUANTITY: ";NA$(I,8)
340 IF NA$(I,9) < > "" THEN PRINT "COMMENT : ";NA$(I,9)
350 GET A$: PRINT : IF A$ = CHR$ (3) THEN J = ND:K = COPI
    ES: GOTO 380
360 BLANK = LL - INT ((LN / LL - INT (LN / LL)) * LL + .0
    5): IF LL = BLANK THEN 380
370 FOR L = 1 TO BLANK: PRINT : NEXT :LN = LN + BLANK
380 NEXT : NEXT : IF PO THEN PRINT CHR$ (4)"PR#0"
390 GOTO 120
400 REM
** CHOICE PARAMETERS **

410 FIND = 1: INPUT "ONE NUMBER ONLY? ";A$: IF LEFT$ (A$,1
    ) = "Y" THEN INPUT "COPIES TO PRINT? ";COPIES: IF COP
    IES < 1 THEN COPIES = 1
420 IF LEFT$ (A$,1) = "Y" THEN 510
430 FIND = 3: VTAB 21: CALL - 958: INPUT "BEGIN AT NUMBER:
```

```
        ";BN: INPUT "END WITH NUMBER: ";EN: IF EN < BN THEN 4
        30
440  GOSUB 630: FOR J = 1 TO NO:I = R(J): IF  VAL (NA$(I,1)
     ) = BN THEN ST = J
450  IF  VAL (NA$(I,1)) = EN THEN ND = J
460  NEXT J
470  IF  VAL (NA$(R(ST),1)) < > BN THEN  VTAB 21: HTAB 20:
      PRINT "INVALID"
480  IF  VAL (NA$(R(ND),1)) < > EN THEN  VTAB 22: HTAB 20:
      PRINT "INVALID"
490  IF  VAL (NA$(R(ST),1)) = BN AND  VAL (NA$(R(ND),1)) =
     EN THEN 230
500  VTAB 23: CALL  - 868: PRINT ">>> ANY KEY RETURNS MENU
     ";: GET A$: PRINT : GOTO 140
510  INPUT "WHICH ID NUMBER? ";ID: GOTO 230
520  FIND = 2: INPUT "WHICH STATE (2 LETTERS)? ";ST$: GOTO 2
     30
530  PO =  NOT PO: GOTO 140
540  FIND = 3: INPUT "START AT RECORD: ";A$:ST =  VAL (A$): IF
     ST < 1 OR (ST > NO) THEN 540
550  INPUT "END WITH RECORD: ";A$:ND =  VAL (A$): IF (ND <
     ST) OR (ND > NO) THEN 550
560  GOTO 230
570  REM
*** SORT CHOICE ***

580  HOME : PRINT "**** SORT ROUTINE FOR ADDRESSES ****": PRINT
     : PRINT : PRINT : PRINT  TAB( 13)"RETURN TO MENU: 0": PRINT

590  PRINT  TAB( 18)"ID NUMBER: 1": PRINT : PRINT  TAB( 23)
     "NAME: 2": PRINT : PRINT  TAB( 23)"CITY: 3": PRINT : PRINT
     TAB( 22)"STATE: 4": PRINT : PRINT  TAB( 24)"ZIP: 5": PRINT

600  PRINT : INPUT "ENTER CHOICE OF SORT FIELD: ";A$:SRT =
     VAL (A$): ON SRT GOTO 630,640,680,690,700: IF SRT THEN
     570
610  GOTO 120
620  REM
*** SET SORT STRING ***

630  FOR I = 1 TO NO:SRT$(I) = NA$(I,1): NEXT :L = 2: GOTO
     710
```

```
640  PRINT "BUILDING SORT KEY....": FOR I = 1 TO NO: FOR J =
     1 TO LEN (NA$(I,2))
650  IF  MID$ (NA$(I,2), LEN (NA$(I,2)) - J,1) = " " THEN K
     = J:J = LEN (NA$(I,2))
660  NEXT J
670  SRT$(I) = RIGHT$ (NA$(I,2),K + 1): NEXT I:L = 1: GOTO
     710
680  FOR I = 1 TO NO:SRT$(I) = NA$(I,6): NEXT :L = 1: GOTO
     710
690  FOR I = 1 TO NO:SRT$(I) = LEFT$ (NA$(I,7),2): NEXT :L
     = 1: GOTO 710
700  FOR I = 1 TO NO:SRT$(I) = RIGHT$ (NA$(I,7),5): NEXT :
     L = 2: GOTO 710
710  REM
*** SORT ROUTINE ***

720  N = NO:M = N
730  M = INT (M / 2):K = N - M:J = 1: PRINT "SORTING ";: IF
     M < > 0 THEN 760
740  PRINT : IF FIND = 3 THEN  RETURN
750  GOTO 120
760  I = J
770  Y = I + M:W = R(I):X = R(Y): ON L GOTO 790: IF  VAL (SR
     T$(W)) < = VAL (SRT$(X)) THEN 810
780  GOTO 800
790  IF SRT$(W) < = SRT$(X) THEN 810
800  Z = R(I):R(I) = R(Y):R(Y) = Z:I = I - M: IF I > = 1 THEN
     770
810  J = J + 1: IF J > K THEN 730
820  GOTO 760
830  REM
*** CHANGE/END ***

840  HOME : PRINT "**** CHANGE ADDRESS LIST ****": PRINT : PRINT
     : PRINT : PRINT  TAB( 9)"RETURN TO MENU: 0": PRINT
850  PRINT  TAB( 12)"ADD ADDRESS: 1": PRINT : PRINT  TAB( 9
     )"CHANGE ADDRESS: 2": PRINT : PRINT  TAB( 9)"DELETE AD
     DRESS: 3": PRINT : PRINT  TAB( 6)"SAVE ADDRESS LIST: 4
     ": PRINT : PRINT  TAB( 15)"FINISHED: 5": PRINT
860  PRINT : INPUT "ENTER CHOICE OF ACTION: ";A$:ACT = VAL
     (A$): ON ACT GOTO 880,960,1190,1250,1370: IF ACT THEN
     830
```

```
870  GOTO 120
880  REM
*** ADD ADDRESS ***

890  N1 = NO + 1: HOME : PRINT "**** ADDING ADDRESS NUMBER "
     ;N1;" ****": PRINT : PRINT : PRINT
900  INPUT "ID NUMBER       :";NA$(N1,1): PRINT : INPUT "NAM
     E LINE #1   :";NA$(N1,2): PRINT
910  INPUT "NAME LINE #2   :";NA$(N1,3): PRINT : INPUT "ADD
     RESS LINE #1:";NA$(N1,4): PRINT
920  INPUT "ADDRESS LINE #2:";NA$(N1,5): PRINT : INPUT "CIT
     Y            :";NA$(N1,6): PRINT
930  INPUT "STATE AND ZIP  :";NA$(N1,7): PRINT : INPUT "QUA
     NTITY LINE  :";NA$(N1,8): PRINT
940  INPUT "COMMENT LINE   :";NA$(N1,9): PRINT
950  PRINT "ANY KEY FOR MENU";: GET A$:NO = N1:R(NO) = NO: GOTO
     120
960  REM
*** CHANGE ADDRESS ***

970  HOME : PRINT "****  CHANGE AN ADDRESS  ****": PRINT "
        (RECORD 0 FOR MENU)": PRINT
980  VTAB 3: HTAB 7: CALL  - 958: INPUT "ENTER RECORD # :";
     J:I = R(J): PRINT :K = 0: IF I < 1 THEN 120
990  IF (I > NO) THEN 980
1000 PRINT "1 ID NUMBER      :";NA$(I,1): PRINT : PRINT "2
     NAME LINE #1   :";NA$(I,2): PRINT
1010 PRINT "3 NAME LINE #2   :";NA$(I,3): PRINT : PRINT "4
     ADDRESS LINE #1:";NA$(I,4): PRINT
1020 PRINT "5 ADDRESS LINE #2:";NA$(I,5): PRINT : PRINT "6
     CITY           :";NA$(I,6): PRINT
1030 PRINT "7 STATE AND ZIP  :";NA$(I,7): PRINT : PRINT "8
     QUANTITY       :";NA$(I,8): PRINT
1040 PRINT "9 COMMENT        :";NA$(I,9): IF ACT = 3 THEN
     RETURN
1050 IF K < > - 1 THEN 1080
1060 PRINT : INPUT " MORE CHANGES?  ";A$: IF  LEFT$ (A$,
     1) = "Y" THEN 980
1070 GOTO 120
1080 PRINT : INPUT " CORRECT RECORD? ";A$: IF  LEFT$ (A$,
     1) < > "Y" THEN 960
```

```
1090 VTAB 23: CALL  - 958: INPUT "  WHICH LINE?      ";K: IF
     K < 1 OR K > 9 THEN 1090
1100 IF K < > 8 THEN  VTAB (3 + 2 * K): HTAB 19: INPUT ""
     ;NA$(I,K):K = - 1: VTAB 5: CALL  - 958: GOTO 1000
1110 IF  LEN (NA$(I,8)) = 0 THEN 1180
1120 NN = 0: FOR K = 1 TO  LEN (NA$(I,8)):J =  ASC ( MID$ (
     NA$(I,8),K,1)): IF J < 46 OR J > 57 THEN NN = 1
1130 NEXT : IF NN = 1 THEN 1180
1140 VTAB 23: CALL  - 958: INPUT "  AMOUNT TO ADD  :";ADD:
     DEC =  VAL (NA$(I,8)) + ADD: IF  ABS (DEC) < .005 THEN
     NA$(I,8) = "":K = - 1: VTAB 5: CALL  - 958: GOTO 1000

1150 IF DEC > 999999 THEN  VTAB 22: CALL  - 868: PRINT "
     AMOUNT TOO LARGE": GOTO 1140
1160 DEC =  SGN (DEC) *  INT ( ABS (DEC) * 100 + .5) / 100:
     NA$(I,8) =  STR$ ( SGN (DEC) * ( ABS (DEC) + .005)):NA
     $(I,8) =  LEFT$ (NA$(I,8), LEN (NA$(I,8)) - 1)
1170 K = - 1: VTAB 5: CALL  - 958: GOTO 1000
1180 VTAB 19: HTAB 19: INPUT "";NA$(I,8):K = - 1: VTAB 5:
     CALL  - 958: GOTO 1000
1190 REM
*** DELETE ADDRESS ***

1200 VTAB 20: INPUT "RECORD NUMBER TO DELETE ";DR:I = R(DR
     ): IF DR < 1 OR (DR > NO) THEN 1200
1210 HOME : PRINT "*** DELETE AN ADDRESS ***": PRINT : PRINT
     : GOSUB 1000
1220 PRINT : INPUT "DELETE THIS RECORD? ";A$: IF  LEFT$ (A
     $,1) < > "Y" THEN 840
1230 VTAB 22: HTAB 21: PRINT "DELETED.": FOR J = 1 TO 500:
     NEXT
1240 FOR J = DR TO NO - 1:R(J) = R(J + 1): NEXT :NO = NO -
     1: GOTO 120
1250 REM
** SAVE ADDRESS LIST **

1260 ONERR  GOTO 1290
1270 PRINT D$"UNLOCK ADD.LIST"
1280 PRINT D$"DELETE ADD.LIST"
1290 POKE 216,0
1300 PRINT D$"OPEN ADD.LIST"
1310 PRINT D$"WRITE ADD.LIST"
```

```
1320  FOR K = 1 TO NO:I = R(K): FOR J = 1 TO 9: PRINT NA$(I
      ,J): NEXT : NEXT
1330  PRINT  CHR$ (4)"CLOSE"
1340  PRINT D$"LOCK ADD.LIST"
1350  IF ACT = 5 THEN  RETURN
1360  GOTO 120
1370  REM
*** FINISHED ***

1380  VTAB 20: HTAB 6: INPUT "SAVE ADDRESS LIST?.";A$: IF  LEFT$
      (A$,1) = "N" THEN 1410
1390  IF  LEFT$ (A$,1) < > "Y" THEN  PRINT : PRINT " ANSWE
      R 'Y' OR 'N' PLEASE": VTAB 20: CALL  - 868: GOTO 1380
1400  GOSUB 1260
1410  PRINT  CHR$ (4)"RUN GRAPE MENU": END
```

Appendix D
Further Reading

Introductions to Personal Computers

The Home Computer Revolution by Theodore H. Nelson, published by the author and available from The Distributors, 702 South Michigan, South Bend, IN 46618. 1978. $2.00. This book is an inexpensive introduction to the world of personal computers by one who saw them coming. It includes some history, technical information, advice about getting started, and discussion of philosophical issues.

Your First Computer by Rodnay Zaks, published by Sybex, 2344 Sixth Street, Berkeley, CA 94710. Second Edition, 1980. $7.95. This is one of the best introductions to the world of personal computer systems. It accomplishes its purpose "to explain what a microcomputer is, how it works, and what it can do, depending upon your intended application and budget." The book is neither technical nor difficult to read.

How to Profit from Your Personal Computer, by T. G. Lewis, published by Hayden Book Company, 50 Essex Street, Rochelle Park, NJ 07662. 1978. $9.65. Lewis's book is for the person ready to deal with the issues of computer applications. He assumes no previous understanding and includes explanations of how to solve real problems using a personal computer.

An Introduction to Microcomputers by Adam Osborne and Jerry Kane, published by Adam Osborne and Associates, Inc., P.O. Box 2036, Berkeley, CA 94702. 1978. In four volumes—$7.95 to $12.99 for each volume. This four-volume set is for the person who wants not only to use computers but to understand them as well. This series of books begins with simple language to explain computers. Volume 0 is "The Beginner's Book" and serves as an excellent introduction not only to the other books of the series but also to computers in general. Volumes 1-3 are more technical and build on Volume 0.

Programming Books

BASIC Programming Primer by Mitchell Waite and Michael Pardee, published by Data Dynamics Technology. 1979. $10.95. This is a good introduction to writing programs in BASIC.

Basic BASIC: An Introduction to Computer Programming in BASIC Language, Second Edition, and

Advanced BASIC: Applications & Problems, both books by James S. Coan, are published by Hayden Book Company, 50 Essex Street, Rochelle Park, NJ 07662. 1978. *Basic BASIC* is $9.45; *Advanced BASIC* is $9.65. This two-book series presents a readable introduction to writing computer programs in BASIC.

The best source of information about the particular dialect of BASIC which your computer uses is the manual which comes with the computer. There are also books and manuals for all high-level languages as well as machine language.

About Computers

Computers and the Cybernetic Society by Michael Arbib, Academic Press, 111 Fifth Avenue, New York, NY 10003. 1977. $15.50. This is one of the best introductions to the potential and actual role of computers. The book deals with a variety of applications and raises some of the philosophical questions which surround computer use.

Man and the Computer by John G. Kemeny, published by Charles Scribner's Sons, New York. 1972. Now out of print but worth finding at a library, this book deals with the issues and potential of computers. As president of Dartmouth College, John Kemeny promoted the writing of BASIC. Although dated in some ways, this book demonstrates the perceptive vision of one of the first prophets of the personal computer age.

Glossary of Computer Terms

This brief glossary is not intended to be a complete dictionary of computer jargon. Its purpose is to clarify words used in this book. For your help in reading, the glossary words have been italicized at their first use in the text. For your help in reference, after each glossary definition I give the page number of either the only or the fullest use of the word in the text.

There are several computer dictionaries available. A small inexpensive dictionary is *Microprocessor Lexicon—Acronyms and Definitions*, edited by Rodnay Zaks and compiled by the staff of Sybex, Berkeley, California, 1978, which costs only $2.95. A more detailed dictionary is *A Dictionary of Microcomputing* by Philip E. Burton, published by Garland Publishing, Inc., 545 Madison Avenue, New York, NY 10022. 1976.

A

Accumulator. The main register in a CPU. In an 8-bit CPU the accumulator is formed of the eight electronic switches used to store the results from the arithmetic and logic unit.   p. 36

Address. See memory address.

Analog. Having a continuous range of electrical information. Analog electronic devices translate information into an analogous electronic form.   p. 32

Arithmetic and Logic Unit. The part of the CPU where logical and mathematical operations are performed.   p. 36

ASCII. An abbreviation for *A*merican *S*tandard *C*ode for *I*nformation *I*nterchange. It is the code used in personal computers for letters and numbers.   p. 34

ASSEMBLY. A computer language which uses mnemonics to replace machine language codes. A very low-level language.   p. 52

B

BASIC. A high-level language developed at Dartmouth College. Personal computers use a dialect of BASIC. There are many forms of BASIC.   p. 41

Baud Rate. The number of individual units of information transmitted in one second. It is measured in bits per second.   p. 27

Benchmark Program. A program designed to assess the relative speed or efficiency of a total computer system.   p. 23

Bit. Contraction of *BI*nary dig*IT*. The smallest unit of information used by a computer. It is one ''on'' or ''off'' switch in computer memory.   p. 34

Bubble Memory. A technology for making memory that offers some promise for future development of inexpensive, large, permanent storage of information.   p. 69

Bus. A set of wires along which the computer transfers information. Often additional electronic circuits can be connected to the bus lines so that the additional circuits have access to the inner workings of the computer.   p. 50

Byte. A set of 8 bits. A byte is used to represent one letter, number, or machine language instruction in a personal computer system.   p. 24

C

Chip. A thin slice cut from a silicon wafer upon which an integrated circuit is printed. Integrated circuits are commonly called chips.   p. 22

Clock. The timing device of a computer. In a computer system the clock provides pulses which trigger or synchronize events.   p. 23

COBOL. *CO*mmon *B*usiness *O*riented *L*anguage. A high-level computer language developed for business applications.   p. 41

Command. A statement written in a carefully constructed upper-level language which tells the computer what to do. A series of commands make up a program.   p. 41

Compiler. A software program which translates a whole program written in a high-level language into machine language code. Either a compiler or interpreter is needed for every high-level language used.   p. 37

Computer. An electronic digital device which is made up of a CPU, memory, and input/output circuits. A computer is connected to other devices such as a terminal and printer to make a computer system.   p. 13

Control Unit. The electronic circuits within the CPU that direct the operation of the CPU.   p. 36

CPS. *C*haracters *P*er *S*econd. A measurement used to designate the working speed of a printer which may vary from fifteen to several hundred CPS.   p. 29

CPU. *C*entral *P*rocessing *U*nit. Includes registers, control unit, and mathematical and logic circuits. The CPU is the brain of the computer.   p. 21

CRT. *C*athode *R*ay *T*ube. The television tube used to display output from a computer. CRT is often used for the terminal which is made from a CRT. Sometimes the terminal is called a VDT (*V*ideo *D*isplay *T*erminal).   p. 23

Cursor. A position indicator used on a CRT to show the position where data is to be entered next.   p. 45

D

Daisy wheel. One kind of printer designed for use with computer systems. Daisy wheel printers are faster than printers using electric typewriter mechanisms.   p. 29

Data. A general term to indicate any number, letter, symbol, or group of numbers, letters, or symbols. Another name for information.   p. 7

Digital. Data that is made up of discrete units. Personal computers use digital data that can be stored in electronic switches which can be either on or off.   pp 32-33

Disk Drive. Hardware used for secondary storage of information for computers. See "Floppy Disk" and "Hard Disk."   p. 26

Dot Matrix. A style of printing in which the figures are made up of individual dots. Printed characters are commonly made up from a matrix of 7 x 7 dots. This is the type of printing often associated with computers; however, computers can also be attached to printing devices which produce type similar to typed or printed characters.   p. 28

Dynamic Memory. An integrated circuit chip which stores information. It has a high density of information but needs to be connected to specially designed electronic circuits which produce regular surges of electricity.   p. 25

E

EPROM. *E*rasable *P*rogrammable *R*ead *O*nly *M*emory. Memory that can be programmed and erased by the user. It retains its content as ROM does until erased with an ultra-violet light.   p. 25

F

Firmware. Software stored in ROM so that it is a permanent part of a computer system.   p. 39

Flat Screen. A possible successor to the CRT as the most common computer input/output device. It is reported to have clearer characters than the CRT and not to cause eye fatigue as quickly when used for a long period of time.   p. 70

Floppy Disk. A mass storage device for computers. Information is stored on a soft plastic disk either 5¼ inches or 8 inches in diameter. The most popular storage method for personal computers.   p. 26

Flowchart. A graphic representation of the logic of a computer program. It is recommended that a flowchart be drawn as an integral step in program development.   p. 43

FORTRAN. *FOR*mula *TRAN*slator. An early high-level language specifically designed for scientific applications. It is available for use on some personal computers.   p. 41

Full Duplex. A communications link between two computers or a computer and a terminal where information is transferred in both directions simultaneously.   p. 30

G

Graphics. The ability of a computer system to produce pictorial representations as well as characters on a CRT or on paper.   p. 25

H

Half Duplex. A communications link between two computers or a computer and a terminal where information can be transferred in only one direction at a time.   p. 30

Hard Copy. Printed material. It is one kind of computer output.   p. 27

Hard Disk. A mass storage device for computers. It is faster and more expensive and stores much more information than a floppy disk.   p. 26

Hardware. Computer equipment. It is part of a total computer system which includes hardware and software.   p. 39

High-Level Language. A programming language which uses statements similar to English sentences. A compiler or interpreter is necessary to translate high-level language statements into machine language. BASIC is an example of a high-level language.   p. 41

Host Computer. In a network system it is the computer which has the primary control.   p. 70

I

Impact Printers. Computer output devices which produce printed material by physically striking an inked ribbon placed on top of paper. Typewriters are impact printers. Impact printers can be dot matrix or letter quality.   p. 27

Input. The programs and data entered into the computer. Also used as a verb meaning the act of entering such information into the computer.   p. 21

Instruction. One line of a program. It tells the computer to accomplish a certain operation.   p. 39

Integrated Circuit. A group of interconnected electronic components manufactured on a silicon chip using a process similar to printing.   p. 22

Interpreter. A software program which translates each statement of a high-level language into machine code before it can be accomplished by the computer. Personal computers contain a BASIC interpreter in ROM.   p. 37

J

JINSAM. The registered trademark of Jini Micro-systems, Inc., for a data base management system for a PET computer.   p. 60

Joy Stick. An input device used to move a dot on a CRT. It is most commonly used for computer games.   p. 30

K

K. The quantity of 1024. It can measure either bits or bytes. 8 K bits equals 8,192 bits while an 8 K memory will have 8,192 bytes of memory (since memory is measured in bytes).   p. 24

Keyboard. The most common input device for computer systems. It usually looks like a typewriter keyboard.   p. 11

L

Letter Quality Printer. A computer output device which produces high quality print. Solid type printers are usually letter quality. Some dot matrix printers are letter quality.   p. 49

Light Pen. An input device used with a CRT. The position of a light shown on the screen is recorded by the computer.   p. 30

List. The sequence of statements that make up a program.   p. 46

M

Machine Language. The set of instructions which are used to direct the operation of the CPU. All high-level languages such as BASIC must be converted into machine language by an interpreter or compiler. Computer programs can be written directly in machine language.   pp. 36-37

Megabyte. 1,024 x 1,024 bytes or about one million bytes.   p. 66

Memory. The part of a computer system where data and programs are stored.   p. 24

Memory address. The electronic code which indicates a specific location in the computer memory. It is often given a numerical value.   p. 25

MHz. *MegaHertz.* One million cycles per second. Units of measurement used for the clock signals that control the operation of the CPU and other parts of the system.   p. 23

Modem. *Mod*ulation/*dem*odulation device. An input/output device which allows computers to communicate over telephone lines.   pp. 29-30

Monitor. A CRT (Cathode Ray Tube) device designed for computer output. Has better resolution than a television screen which can also be used for computer output. See also system monitor.   p. 23

N

Network. An interconnection of computers and terminals. Often a network will include a large, shared data base.   p. 70

Non-impact printers. Computer output devices that produce printed material without physically striking the paper. They are usually much faster than impact printers. Non-impact printers include printers which spray ink onto paper and printers that use a thermal process.   p. 27

O

Output. The information which is produced by the computer and sent to a device where it can be stored or inspected. CRTs and printers are the most common output devices.   p. 21

P

Parallel Interface. The fastest way to transfer information from one device to another because individual wires are used to move one byte each.   p. 34

PASCAL. A high-level programming language which is gaining popularity with personal computer programmers.   p. 41

Peripheral Devices. Any computer hardware that can be attached to a CPU. Peripherals include printers, light pens, and joy sticks.   p. 21

Printed Circuit Board. The fiberglass or pressed paper sheet used for mounting computer circuits. Some computer systems use individual boards for memory circuits, input/output circuits, and other functions.   p. 55

Program Counter. A register in the CPU where the computer records the memory address of the next instruction.   p. 36

Program. To write the series of instructions (software) for a computer; also, the series of instructions written for a computer.   pp. 41 *ff*

PROM. *P*rogrammable *R*ead *O*nly *M*emory. ROM memory which can be permanently programmed by the user.   p. 25

R

RAM. *R*andom *A*ccess *M*emory. Specifically the random access memory where the contents can be set by the program. RAM is a necessary part of all computer systems.   pp. 24-25

Real Time Clock. Part of a computer system that keeps track of the passage of time. It is an optional part of a computer system.   p. 56

Register. A set of on and off switches found in the CPU. It is used to store data and memory addresses necessary for the functioning of the CPU. See accumulator and program counter.   p. 36

RF Modulator. Converts output signals from a computer into a form that can be received by an ordinary television screen.   p. 23

ROM. *R*ead *O*nly *M*emory. The content of this memory is set when the ROM chip is manufactured. Its content is not destroyed when the electric power is turned off as happens with most RAM. Personal computers include a BASIC interpreter in ROM.   p. 25

S

S-100 Bus. A popular standardized system of connecting parts of a computer system to the CPU. The S-100 boards from various manufacturers can be combined to build a computer system.   p. 50

SCRIPSIT/DISK. The registered trademark of Tandy Corporation for a software package for word processing with a TRS-80 microcomputer.   pp. 52-53

Secondary Storage. Storage beyond the RAM and ROM of a computer system. Floppy disks, hard disks, and cassette recorders are examples of secondary storage devices.   pp. 25-26

Serial Interface. When a single wire is used to transfer information between devices in a computer system.   p. 34

Solid Type Printer. A printer that produces print similar in quality to that produced on an electric typewriter.   p. 28

Software. The set of instructions (programs) which make the computer system work. Software and hardware (computer equipment) make up a computer system.   p. 39

Static Memory. An integrated circuit chip (RAM) which stores information. It does not lose its content as long as power is applied.   p. 25

String Variable. A series of characters (either numbers of letters) considered to be one block of information by the computer. In BASIC string variables are indicated with the sign $.   p. 46

System Monitor. The program contained in ROM which controls the operation of the computer system.   p. 25

T

Terminal. Any device which has input and output capabilities. CRTs are the most common terminals; however, some terminals produce hard copy output and do not use a CRT.   p. 11

Thermal Printers. Printers used for computer output which are non-impact and use heat and a specially treated paper.   p. 27

Time-Sharing. A system where many users share a common CPU and data base. Because computers process information so quickly, many users can use the computer at the same time yet each be given the impression that the computer is working only for him or her.   p. 11

V

Video Disk. A technology which may produce an inexpensive way to provide large amounts of random access computer readable data for personal computer owners.   pp. 69-70

VISICALC. The registered trademark of Personal Software, Inc. for a software package which makes it possible to analyze budgets and make financial projections.   p. 40

W

WORD PRO. The registered trademark of Professional Software for a software package for word processing with a PET computer.   p. 55

Word Processing System. The software and hardware which make it possible for a computer to assist with the production of written material.   p. 16